SUBURBAN LEEDS

A comparison of Headingley, Woodhouse, Burley and Kirkstall as Suburbs of Modern Leeds (1949-1981)

By Carol Winteringham

Published by ThreePeppers Publishing

Copyright © 2022 Carol Winteringham
Copyright © 2022 ThreePeppers Publishing

Carol Winteringham has asserted her right under the Copyright, Designs and Patents Act, 1988, to be identified as the author of this work.

All rights reserved. No part of this book shall be reproduced, stored in a retrieval system, or transmitted by any means – electronic, mechanical, photocopying, recording, or otherwise – without written permission from the author and the publisher.

1st Edition – January 2022
ISBN: 9781838494353

Cover:
A map of Leeds, England in 1866 by J Bartholemew, distributed under a CC-BY 2.0 license

www.3peppers.co.uk

To my Mum and Dad

Contents

List of Maps, Diagrams and Figures 9
Foreword 13
Introduction 15
Chapter 1: Location of the Four Suburbs 17
Chapter 2: The Residential Development Pattern of the Four Suburbs 25
Chapter 3: Differentiation of the Four Suburbs 31
Chapter 4: Industry in the Suburbs of Woodhouse and Kirkstall 37
Chapter 5: Urbanisation 55
Chapter 6: Slum Clearance 63
Chapter 7: Urban Renewal and Development 69
Chapter 8: The Shopping Facilities 89
Chapter 9: Conclusions 125
Appendices 127
Acknowledgements 133
Bibliography 135

List of Maps, Diagrams and Figures

Map 1 18
Map 2 22
Map 3 23
Map 4 27
Map 5 28
Map 6 29
Map 7 39
Figure 8 40
Map 9 41
Map 10 43
Map 11 46
Map 12 47
Map 13 48
Map 14 49
Map 15 50
Map 16 52
Map 17 57
Map 18 58
Map 19 59
Map 20 60
Map 21 61
Map 22 67
Map 23 71
Map 24 72
Map 25 74

Figure 25	75
Map 26	85
Map 27	87
Map 28	91
Map 29	93
Map 30	94
Map 31	95
Map 32	96
Map 33	97
Map 34	98
Map 35	99
Map 36	100
Map 37	101
Map 38	102
Map 39	107
Map 40	108
Map 41	109
Map 42	110
Map 43	111
Map 44	112
Map 45	113
Map 46	114
Map 47	115
Map 48	116
Map 49	117
Map 50	118
Map 51	120

Map 52 121
Map 54 123
Map 55 124

Foreword

It is now 2021. This dissertation is over 50 years old. It is something I wrote while I was studying to become a school teacher as part of my final studies. It takes into consideration the housing, industry, and shopping facilities in four northern suburbs in the city of Leeds. It looks back at their historical development but concentrates on the situation up to 1968 as well as future plans up to 1981. At the time when this was written there were no computers or the Internet, so everything was painstakingly written by hand and information about the shops and industries was gathered first hand. Looking back, I must have walked miles to complete the maps explaining the types of shops and industries. This area of Leeds is completely different today and has developed even further, so many places or street names may no longer exist. I decided to put this work to print as I hope this study may prove useful to curious students or just be interesting reading for those of you who know this part of Leeds.

Carol Winteringham

Introduction

My home town is Leeds and I live in the suburb of Headingley. Leeds is a large complex city comprising of several suburbs, originally known as Out-Townships.

In this study the aim is to consider the modern development of four of these suburbs. There are a large number of suburbs to choose from, several of which have developed at remarkable speed during the past few years, such as Seacroft. However, this study will concentrate on suburbs within my immediate home area: Headingley, Woodhouse, Burley and Kirkstall, so as to study adequately in this field.

These four areas are well established suburbs of Leeds and unlike the modern suburbs of towns which are concise, separate units, these suburbs have become mingled, and it is decidedly difficult to establish where one suburb ends and another begins.

The only common factor linking them together is that they are all very old parts of Leeds; as we shall see later, all of these four parts are included in the zone of older housing. However, these four suburbs are included in Leeds City Council's Review of the Developmental Plan (1961-1981). The planning considered industry, housing, shopping facilities, routeways and transport.

This study is examining the four suburbs at a very interesting stage of development. It is now 1968 to 1969 that we are beginning to see some of the fruits of their planning.

The study aims to indicate the overall plan for the four suburbs up to 1981, but what is more important is that it shows the situation at present. It presents the ideal and the realistic. I hope this will reveal several problems to the geographer - involving slums, rate of slum clearance, influx of students and immigrants and the rate of development.

In conclusion, the study will be concerned with whether the planners will be successful in their re-development and improvement plans of the four suburbs in relation to other factors such as the "age" of the area and people's preference for the modern suburbs of Leeds; the areas under study are rapidly becoming dominated by immigrants, students, and poorer families.

Is this a declining part of Leeds?

The suburbs have all developed differently and for a different purpose, so to study them some historical background must be included, to give insight as to what each suburb originated for. The differentiation of the suburbs will be introduced in a separate chapter which will include a little history, whereas the main part of the historical information and background can be found at the end of the study in the Appendices. The study, whilst looking at the development of the four suburbs from 1949 to 1981 and attempting to grasp the situation at present, revealing several developmental problems, it will have a central theme of the differences in the suburbs. The differentiation will be made through comparison, in terms of how the development is different for each suburb and the differing rates of development. Some areas in the suburbs have been developed far more than others. In order to make a reasonable comparison of the suburbs, they will not be considered individually. There will be chapters dealing with the main issues of suburbia, such as housing and shopping facilities and all the suburbs will be compared against each other, in each issue.

Chapter 1: Location of the Four Suburbs

All of the four suburbs under study, Woodhouse, Kirkstall, Burley and Headingley are to be located on the North and North-west side of the city of Leeds, as can be seen from Map1. Also, in Map 1 and in the Block Diagram in Map 2 it is evident that the four suburbs are all next to each other, in a concise area.

Map 1 shows the Medieval Townships of Leeds and from the Map it can be seen that apart from Woodhouse, the suburbs under study originally formed one township; this was the Headingley Township.

Firstly, let us take a look at the odd one out which is Woodhouse (as in Map 1). In the past, from Medieval Times to about the late 19th Century, Woodhouse was part of the Leeds Central Area, it belonged to the In-Township of Leeds. Moving Northwards out of the city Great Woodhouse was the first residential area to be crossed. In fact, it was the only residential area in the In-Townships of Leeds. However, after urbanization when Woodhouse became densely housed, the Central Leeds Area was given a new boundary. The new area was an area solely for industry, Business and Culture – having no residential parts. Woodhouse became the first residential suburb or neighbourhood to cross as one travels north out of the city centre. Of the four suburbs it is the most Northerly.

Continuing out of Woodhouse in a North westerly direction, the next suburb is Headingley. Hyde Park is a small unit which acts as a link between Woodhouse and Headingley, as in Map 2. From Map 1, in Medieval Times Burley did not exist, but Headingley existed. It was an Out-Township of Leeds. Travelling in a North westerly direction it was the first Out Township after the Leeds In–Township. Headingley extended North-westward. The most westerly part and furthest from the central area was West Headingley and the other was East Headingley. Today, East Headingley is referred to as Headingley and the westerly part as Far Headingley. See Map 2. Completely west, in the In–Township of Headingley we had Kirkstall; this was the Abbey and grounds. Burley still did not exist.

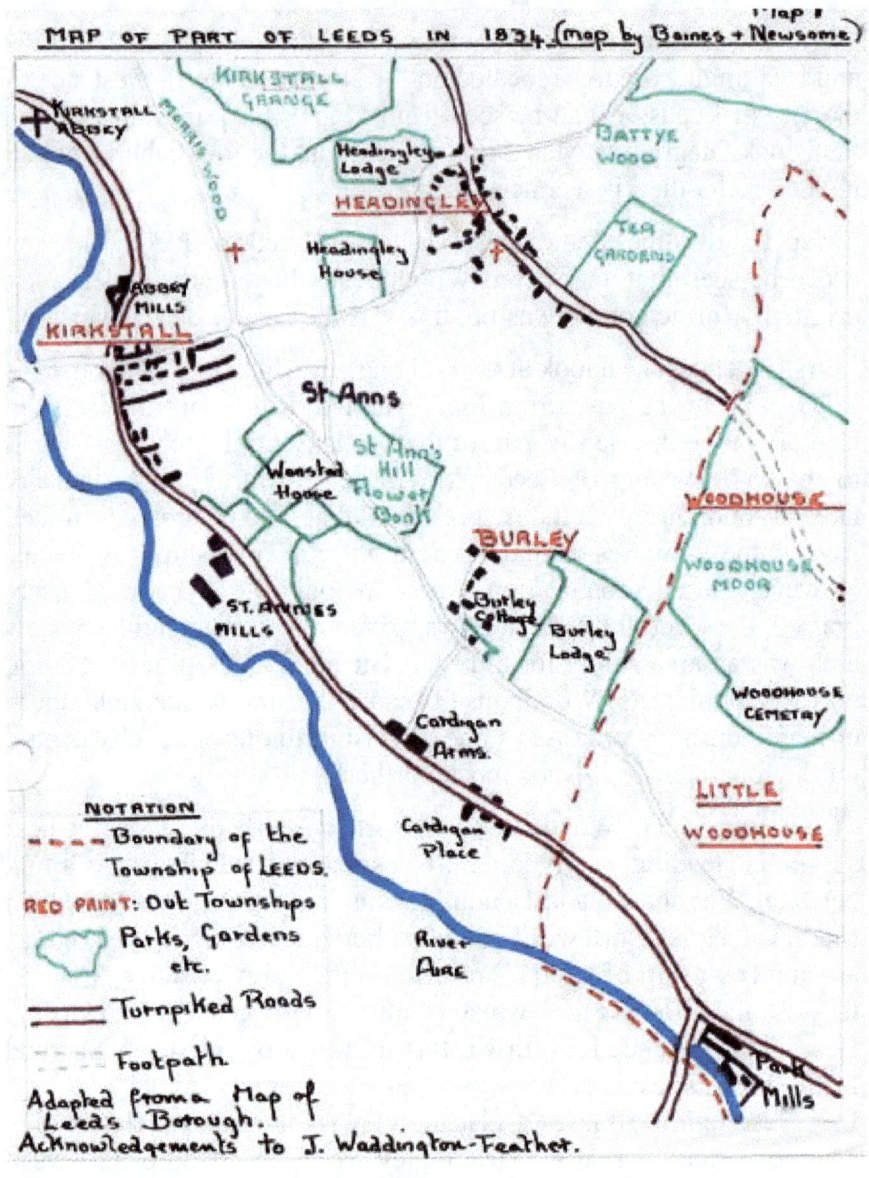

Map 1

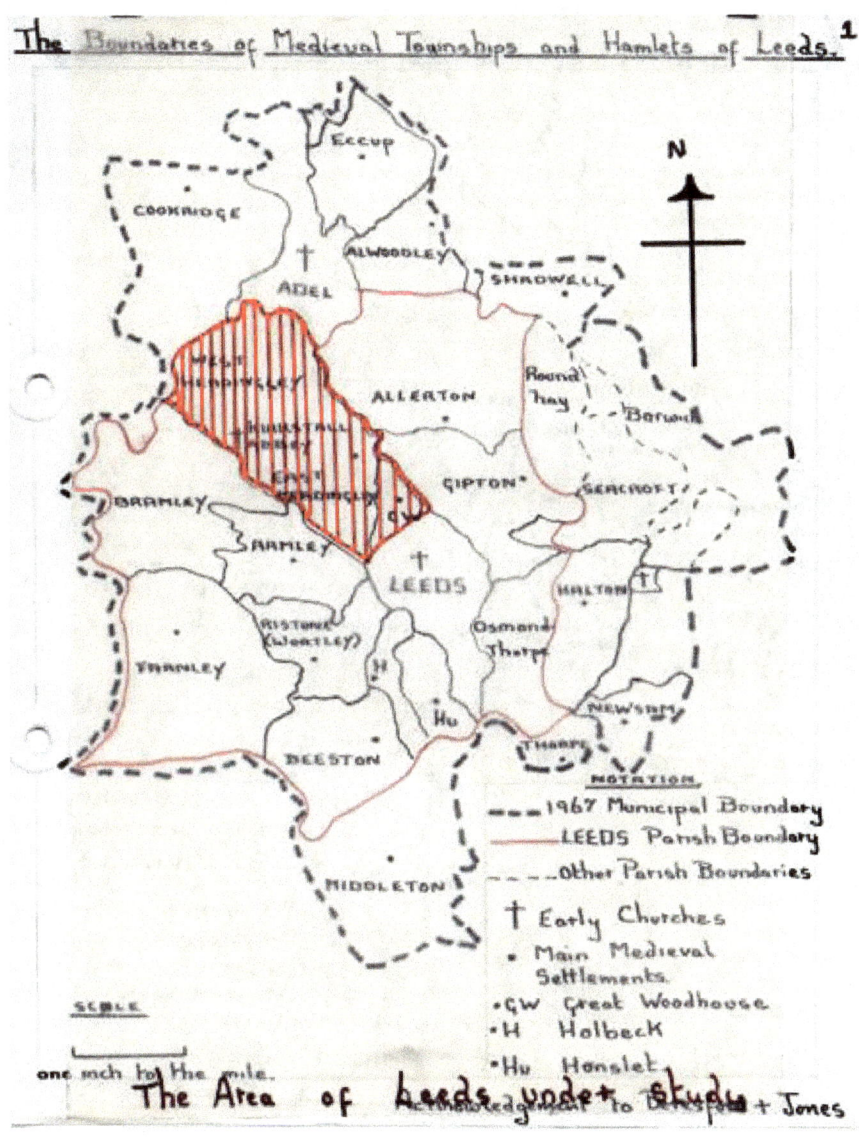

Map 1B

Map 1C

Headingley has virtually the same location today. It extends in a North West direction and is bounded by Allerton to the East, Lawnswood leading to Adel and Cookridge in the North and North west, see Map 2.

Kirkstall is the most Westerly of the suburbs, but it does not extend westerly because this suburb is bounded by the River Aire, the Leeds and Liverpool Canal and the Railway. Instead, Kirkstall extends in a Northerly pattern parallel to the River, Canal and Road and Railway. On the other side of these communications is the suburb of Bramley. Southerly, Kirkstall leads into the Leeds City Central Area.

Burley is the easiest suburb to locate because it is the central suburb, with all the other suburbs surrounding it; see Map 2. In the following chapter we will see how Burley came to be in such a central position.

Map 3 aims to show an attempt to fit the study area into a "region" which shows another way of locating the suburbs. Woodhouse, Burley, Kirkstall and Headingley are all residential suburbs which fit into an area between two valley systems: the Meanwood Valley and the Aire Valley.

Meanwood Valley is in the East and the Aire Valley in the West. Although Meanwood Valley is not actually part of my study, it and the Aire Valley provide a sort of limitation or boundary to the area under study.

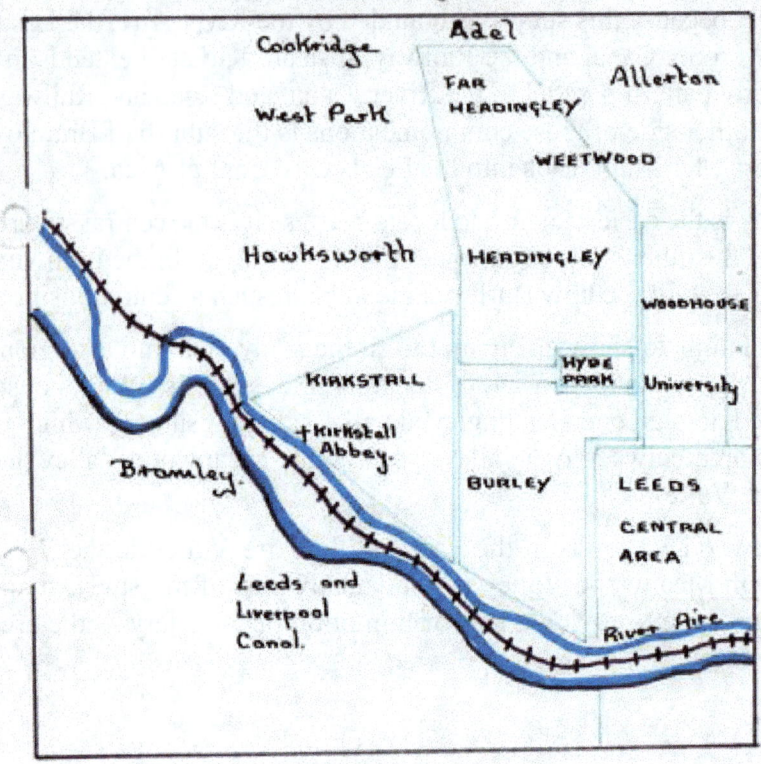

Map 2

A Diagramatic Map showing how the studied area of Leeds fits into a concise, organised region.

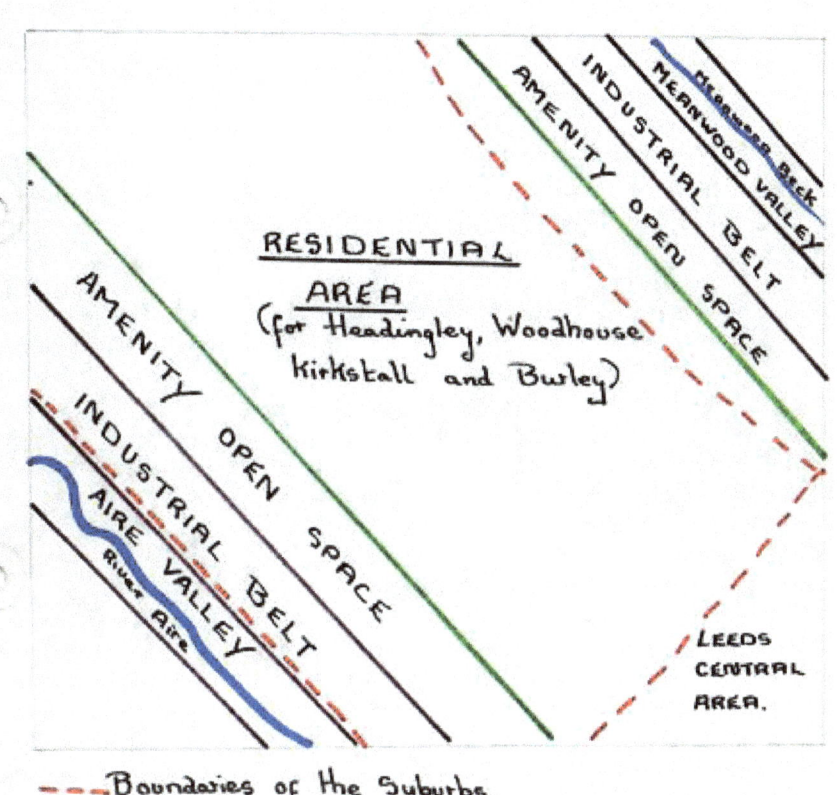

Map 3

Chapter 2: The Residential Development Pattern of the Four Suburbs

The residential development of Leeds began naturally from the town centre. During the Industrial Revolution large factories and businesses formed in the Central Area, driving the more wealthy people out of the inner city. The wealthy wanted to be out of reach of the factories and smoke. They began to move out of the Leeds In-Township onto high ground out of the Industrial valleys. In Leeds, the higher ground is on the North and North West side of the city.

As residential areas developed out of the In Township, they tended to follow the turnpike road systems that travelled in a North and North Westerly direction.

Kirkstall developed along the turnpike road leading out to Guiseley and Rawdon.

Woodhouse extended along the Skipton turnpike road. As development continued these suburbs spread outward from the road, as in Map 4 Stage 1.

Urbanisation was so great that housing spread across the intervening district between Woodhouse and Kirkstall. This led to the formation of the suburb of Burley, linking the three suburbs into a completely built up area, as in Map 4. This rapid development took place toward the end of the 1800s and was a period known as Urbanisation. See Map 5 and 6.

Headingley was the last suburb to be residentially developed because it was not owned by the Leeds Corporation but by the wealthy industrialists and so building was done privately and selectively. Parts of Headingley especially Far Headingley did not develop until 1930 and after. However, Headingley mainly developed in the early 1900s spreading further along the Skipton turnpike road. Those parts that developed from 1930 onward are in a period known as sub-urbanisation. See Map 5 and 6.

Map 5 and 6 Growth rings illustrate how Leeds developed. Each ring forming a new area of development and Map 6 indicates the type of development.

Growth rings are a valuable way of marking the development of large cities and they give a clear illustration of the development pattern in Leeds.

From historical data it is evident that the 19th century was the time when these suburbs, as indeed the whole of Leeds, grew extensively. As can be seen from Map 4 housing development began by spreading along the radial turnpike road system, then with urbanization it spread back from the road and eventually across the intervening districts, creating a completely urbanized area.

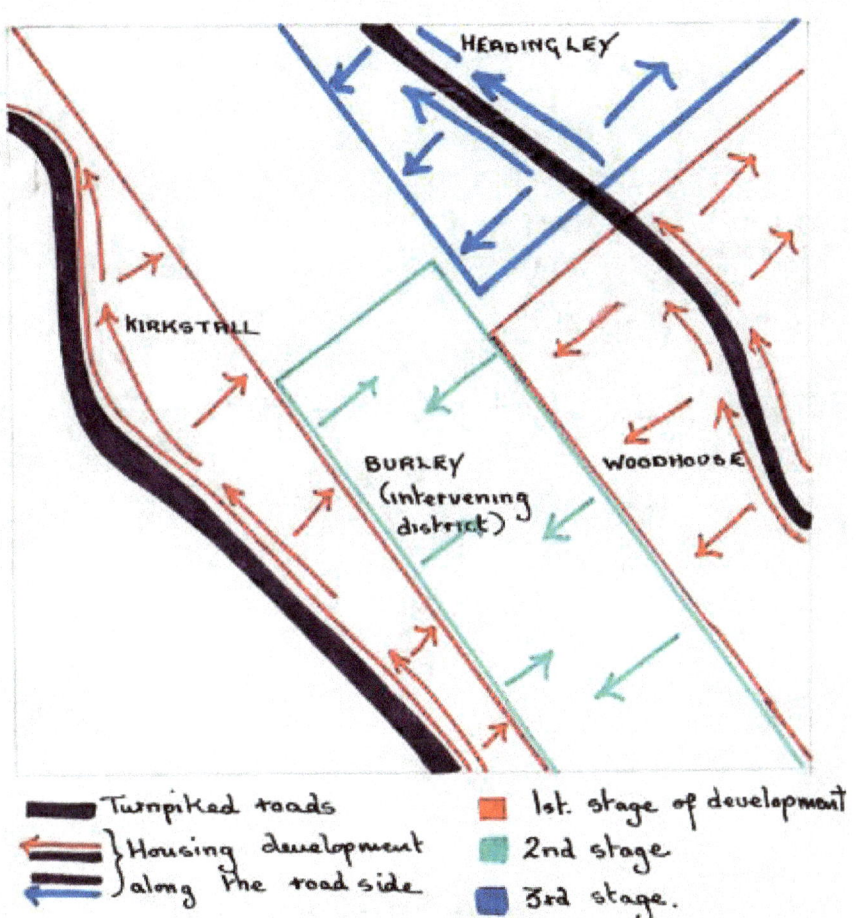

Map 4

HISTORICAL GROWTH RINGS OF LEEDS
(including Woodhouse, Kirkstall, Burley + Headingley)

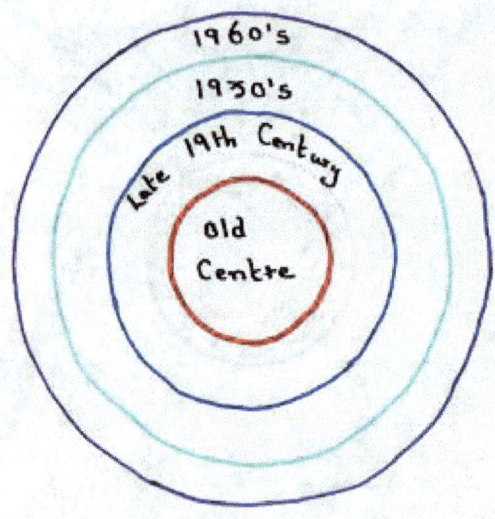

Acknowledgements to Hilary Rose
and "The Housing Problem"

Map 5

URBANISATION RINGS OF LEEDS
(including Kirkstall, Burley, Woodhouse + Headingley)

- RECENT SUB-URBANISATION
- SUB-URBANISATION
- URBANISATION
- CENTRE Solely for Business, Industry + Culture

<u>URBANISATION</u>: Dense Working Class Housing WOODHOUSE, KIRKSTALL, BURLEY.

<u>SUB-URBANISATION</u>: "made by the richer strata of town dwellers seeking the outer edge to escape the congestion and overcrowding of the central area." HEADINGLEY.

<u>RECENT SUB-URBANISATION</u>: Private and Local Authority Estates (Housing and Flats)

Adapted from the Historical Growth Rings in H. Rose's "The Housing Problem"

Map 6

Chapter 3: Differentiation of the Four Suburbs

In order to explain the differences among Woodhouse, Headingley, Kirkstall and Burley I shall begin at the time of the Industrial Revolution, because that was the period when any real urbanization or growth began.

GREAT WOODHOUSE is situated in the North West corner of the In Township of Leeds. It is situated on the flank of a ridge (today known as Woodhouse Ridge). The valley acts as a routeway and leads into Leeds city centre. This valley is not part of Woodhouse but of Meanwood.

A domestic cloth industry had established itself in Meanwood Valley. With the Industrial Revolution came the North Eastern Railway through Leeds, the Leeds–Liverpool Canal and steam power bringing a change to Leeds industry, especially the woollen industry. Large factories were set up along Meanwood Road in the Valley and several factories spread into Woodhouse, as overspills of Meanwood. A turnpike network of roads was made from Leeds for the conveyance of wool, woollen goods, and dye stuffs; two important turnpiked roads were Meanwood Road travelling to Harrogate and the road North West, through Woodhouse to Skipton, via Otley. Other industries developed in Meanwood Valley; these were wholesale clothing factories, dyeworks and tanneries. Industry and Commerce developed rapidly in Leeds centre and the wealthy factory owners and industrialists who had resided in the township now wished to move away from the large chimneyed factories, the smoke and grime. The majority of these wealthy people moved to live in houses and villas in Woodhouse. Woodhouse was in an ideal position; it was an In-Township close to industry and business but also sufficiently on the outskirts of the town to be residential for the rich. Large houses and detached villas were built on the hill slope of Woodhouse ridge, built on the higher ground so as to be out of the smoke and grime of the Industrial valleys. This more wealthy part of Woodhouse became known as Little Woodhouse. In the 1800s it became a high class suburb. A new Grammar school was built in 1859, the Yorkshire College was built in 1885 which marked the beginning of Leeds University.

Many houses of the "high class" era of Woodhouse still remain in the University precinct; for example, "Claremont" in Clarendon Road, and "Beech Grove" where today we have the University's Department of Education. Woodhouse was also given a covered–in reservoir, a cemetery, a zoo, and botanical gardens. Also in 1855 Woodhouse Moor, still a popular park was bought by Leeds Corporation in order to provide more open space in the In-Township. These things give evidence to the wealth and class of this suburb at the time. So, Woodhouse became residentially popular among the rich and housing gradually spread along the turnpike road via Otley to Skipton.

Industry continued to develop in Meanwood Valley and in that part of Great Woodhouse that linked to Meanwood; housing was urgently required for the large number of workers. In Fowler's Plan 1821, housing plans were made for working class houses, back to backs and narrow streets were built in the area and spread along North Road and Camp Road into Woodhouse. This rapid extension, westward of working class houses was the main factor that limited the period of tie of Woodhouse as a "high class" suburb; the working class housing and villas of the rich were getting closer to each other; they were becoming one. Woodhouse had its hey- day but in a short time the wealthy owners were selling their villas and moving out of the industrial Township into Out–Townships. Woodhouse became a working class suburb.

HEADINGLEY was the first immediate Out–Township after the Leeds In-Township. Headingley was a relatively small place in the early 1800s, with just a few buildings, but in the 1860s when the rich were forced out of Woodhouse, a large number came to live in Headingley.

Headingley was an Out–Township to the North of Leeds and on

higher ground therefore it was away from the industry and dirt, suitable for the wealthy. They settled in an area known as Headingley Hill and along the turnpike road to Skipton.

Woodhouse had a little industry of its own and suitable housing for its workers and being an In-Township, it was close to Leeds industry.

However, Headingley was an Out-Township unblemished by industrial factories and workers houses and so it gradually developed into a purely residential suburb presided by doctors, bankers, factory owners and business men in general. Many business men set up private businesses, mainly shops and banks in Headingley for the rich. Headingley took the place of Woodhouse in becoming a high class suburb of Leeds with its large houses, small private shops, and banks. It was a concise, almost independent unit.

The more wealthy you were, the further away from the Leeds In-Township you went to live. More and more large houses were built far out of Leeds in West Headingley, known today as Far Headingley reaching into another suburb, Adel.

The residential pattern then began with living in the town centre, growing outward North and Northwestward on higher ground and stretching outward along road systems.

KIRKSTALL is the only industrial suburb of the four, under study. Even from early times there had always been domestic industries in Kirkstall set up by the Cistercian monks at Kirkstall Abbey. It was during the Industrial Revolution that Kirkstall had a sudden boom in industry because of its natural position being advantageous for industry,

Kirkstall is situated near the Leeds and Liverpool Canal and the River Aire was made navigable to Leeds at the end of the 17thCentury. So, being in proximity to the river, the canal and later the railway, there was ample scope for the transport for heavy goods such as coal and iron. Iron and metal work industries began alongside the river and canal route. There were many heavy engineering works, such as Kirkstall Forge which at this present time, is still yielding a good output.

The textile industry, especially the weaving of cloth, became popular in Kirkstall Valley. There was availability of wool, coal for power, also water for power as well as other textile processes in close proximity and there were also adequate means of transport. Also, in this area there was a group of experienced Irish weavers who were able to advance the industry.

Kirkstall and the Aire Valley was worked to the full in the 1800s. In Leeds at the time there were three main areas where industry was concentrated: 1) Kirkstall and the Aire Valley, 2) Meanwood Valley, 3) Hunslet and Holbeck. Leeds relied on these three areas for their industrial, economic stability so we can appreciate the intensity of industrialization there must have been in Kirkstall. With this intensity there arose a similar situation to the one in Woodhouse and Meanwood, working class houses were urgently required. Such houses were built along the turnpike road going to Skipton through Rawdon via Kirkstall. At the time when these houses were built, before 1900, there was no official control over the building of working class houses, the result was that rows and rows of back to back houses in narrow streets were built, interwoven with factories and warehouses.

Even today, in Kirkstall where demolition has not yet taken place, one can still clearly see the mingling of factories and back to back houses; it is an extremely intense industrial area. Working class houses could not extend West due to the River Aire and the Leeds and Liverpool Canal so it spread Eastward which led to the formation of another suburb called Burley.

BURLEY had previously been just a small green district containing a large estate owned by Lord Cardigan and when so much working class housing was needed, he sold that part of the estate nearest Kirkstall so more houses could be built. Lord Cardigan's park land was kept intact and became Burley Park, as it is known today. A Zoo and Botanical Gardens were going to be built on Cardigan Road. The housing spread Eastward around the park until it eventually joined with Woodhouse and Headingley suburbs.

It is evident that each suburb has developed differently. Kirkstall, Woodhouse and Burley were all part of the Industrial boom and at the same time they were all residential, having suffered dense urbanization. They became units of rows and rows of back-to-back houses in narrow streets, but Kirkstall also became an important concentrated industrial suburb of Leeds, and it has remained so to this day.

Headingley, however, was not so densely populated as the other three because it was owned by the wealthy who made it into a select suburb of Leeds using different building criteria but later in the 1900s more intense housing development did commence.

Summary of the Differentiation

HEADINGLEY:

- Purely residential for the wealthy people of Leeds
- Development was private and select not part of the Urbanization
- Development in parts was as late as 1930

WOODHOUSE:

- Originally residential, but its proximity to Leeds In-Township and the influence of industrial development in Leeds centre itself as well as the Meanwood Valley, made it a part of the Urbanisation in the late 19th Century, dense, working class and clothing factories.

KIRKSTALL:

- Mainly industrial due to its position and natural advantages that is the River Aire, The Leeds and Liverpool Canal, the railway; Industrial as from Medieval times due to the Monastery but development came during the Industrial Revolution
- Intense industrialization took place, leading to the building of densely populated working class houses intermixed with the factories

BURLEY:

- Developed solely to provide urgently required working class housing for Kirkstall factory workers

Chapter 4: Industry in the Suburbs of Woodhouse and Kirkstall

The reasons for Industry in Kirkstall and its development during the Industrial Revolution can be found in the appendices.

The North and North-West side of Leeds is not considered to be an industrial part of Leeds; the major industrial belts have always been in the South and South East Leeds. It is to remain so in the future as can be seen from Map7 on the next page. The North and North-West side is more residential, because of its physical relief on high ground. However, this part of Leeds is not devoid of industry completely. The two areas where industries are concentrated are Woodhouse and Kirkstall.

The suburb of Kirkstall is an industrial Belt in itself, but Woodhouse is only on the edge of the industrial belt of Meanwood, therefore there is not a mass of factories but an overspill of a few factories, where Meanwood Road and Woodhouse Street join.

Kirkstall is very different from the other three suburbs because it is the only true industrial suburb of the four and it has been such since its beginnings in the 1100s. During the Industrial Revolution Kirkstall developed its Iron and Metal work industries, Textile industries, Tanneries as well as other small local businesses.

Iron and metal work, textiles and tanning were the three main types of industry in Kirkstall, and they were also the main industries found in Leeds generally. These three industries remain in Leeds Industrial production today.

The situation of industry in Kirkstall today is complicated to assess because we must look at the way it is today and establish the similarities with its state during the Industrial Revolution. The Leeds City Council's Plan Review consider Kirkstall one of the main industrial belts, as from 1961 to 1981, and is undergoing many changes, industrial changes that we must take a look at.

At present, the appearance of the industrial belt, stemming along the banks of the River Aire and Kirkstall Road is one of deteriorating dirty factories that have been overworked since industrialization began. From looking at the industries on Maps 9 to 11, there is still evidence of the types of industry flourishing in the period of industrialization, similar to the types found today.

MILLS: Namely, Aire Place Mills, Map 10, St. Anne's Mills, Map 34, and Abbey Mills. These were originally cloth weaving mills but now each one has taken on a different use, mainly metal and engineering works.

IRON AND METAL WORK: As previously stated there was an intensity in this branch of industry in industrial times. The situation remains almost the same today and it is increasing in importance. One extremely large firm, J. Woodhouse and Sons on Map 9, was established in 1850 and today has a worldwide organization, dealing in metal work for railway rolling stock and road vehicles – see Figure 8.

TANNING/LEATHER WORK: this stems from industrial times but today it is decreasing in importance in Kirkstall. The Oak Tannery on Map10(2) began in 1876 and is still quite prosperous today, although it is the only tannery left in Kirkstall.

PRINTING: This is quite an important industry in Kirkstall as we can establish from the graph in figure 15 and it is also an important proportion of the Leeds Printing industry.

The city of Leeds is important for all these four types of industry, so although Kirkstall appears dirty and deteriorating, it is justifiably contributing to Leeds industry as a whole.

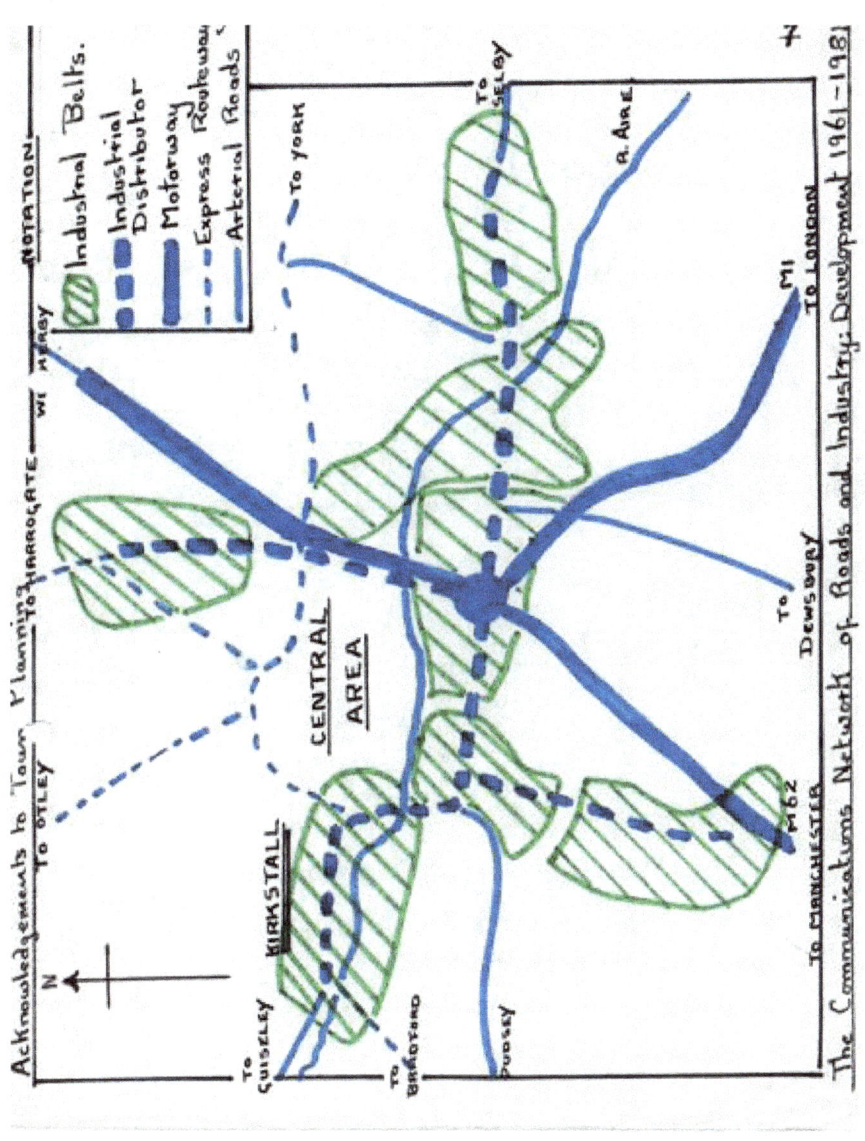

Map 7

WOODHEADS OF LEEDS
SPAN THE
WORLD

PRODUCTS

LAMINATED SPRINGS—RAILWAY ROLLING STOCK
LAMINATED SPRINGS—ROAD VEHICLES
COIL SPRINGS
SMALL SPRINGS—Compression, Tension, Torsion and Flat
SHOCK ABSORBERS (Telescopic Type) RAILWAY ROLLING STOCK
SHOCK ABSORBERS (Telescopic Type) ROAD VEHICLES
SHOCK ABSORBERS (Lever Type)
TORSION AND ANTI-ROLL BARS
DISC SPRINGS
STARTER GEAR RINGS
FORGING
PRESSWORK
MACHINING
FABRICATION
HOLLOW STEEL
RE-ROLLING
STRUCTURAL STEELWORK
CABLE TRUNKING, TRAYS AND BUS-BAR SYSTEMS
AGRICULTURAL BUILDINGS AND CATTLE GRIDS
CONVEYORS AND ELEVATORS
'CAREFREE' TRAYS AND TROLLEYS
CONVEYOR BELT IDLERS
MOTOR BODY IRONWORK
SPRING REPAIR SERVICES

World Wide Organisation

Head Office:-
JONAS WOODHEAD & SONS LTD.
KIRKSTALL ROAD - LEEDS 4

Figure 8

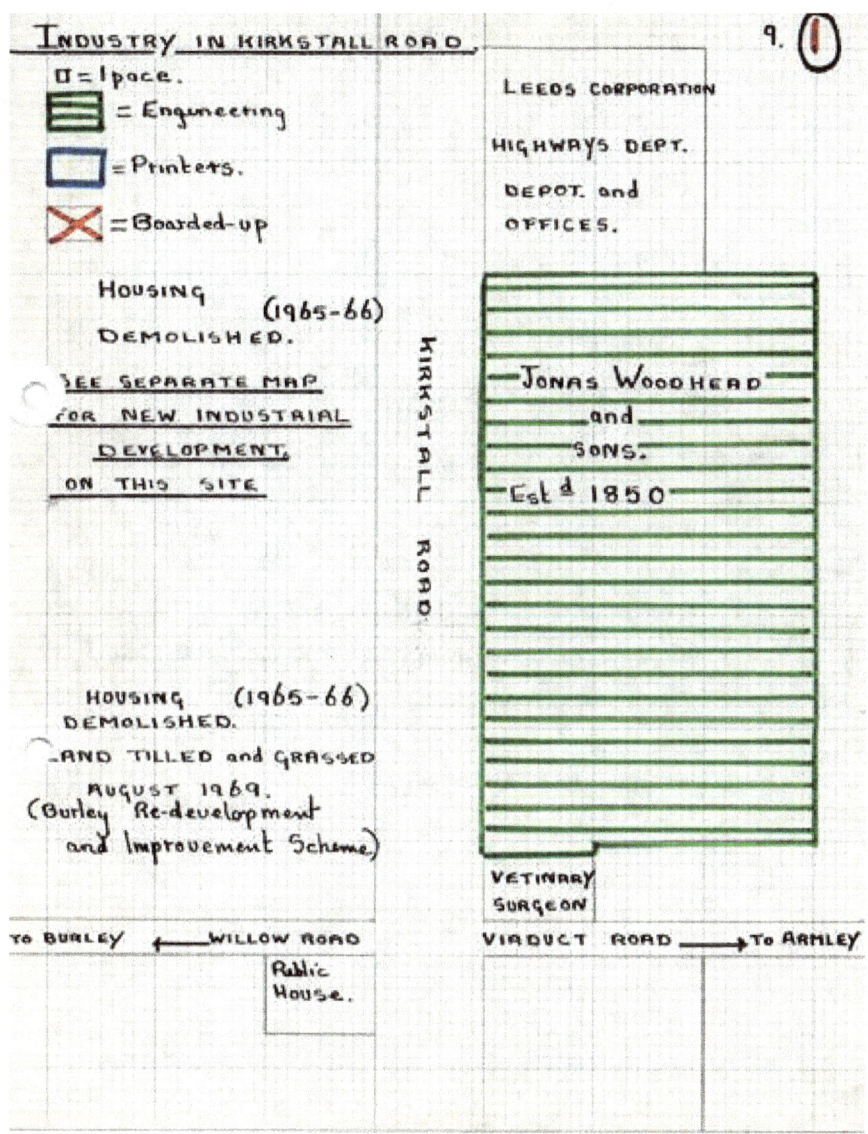

Map 9

NOTATION TO INDUSTRY

☐ ENGINEERING

☐ PRINTING

☐ WOOLLEN + CLOTHING

☐ JOINERY + BUILDING

☐ NEW LIGHT INDUSTRIES (Electrical Factors)

☒ INDUSTRIES BOARDED-UP.

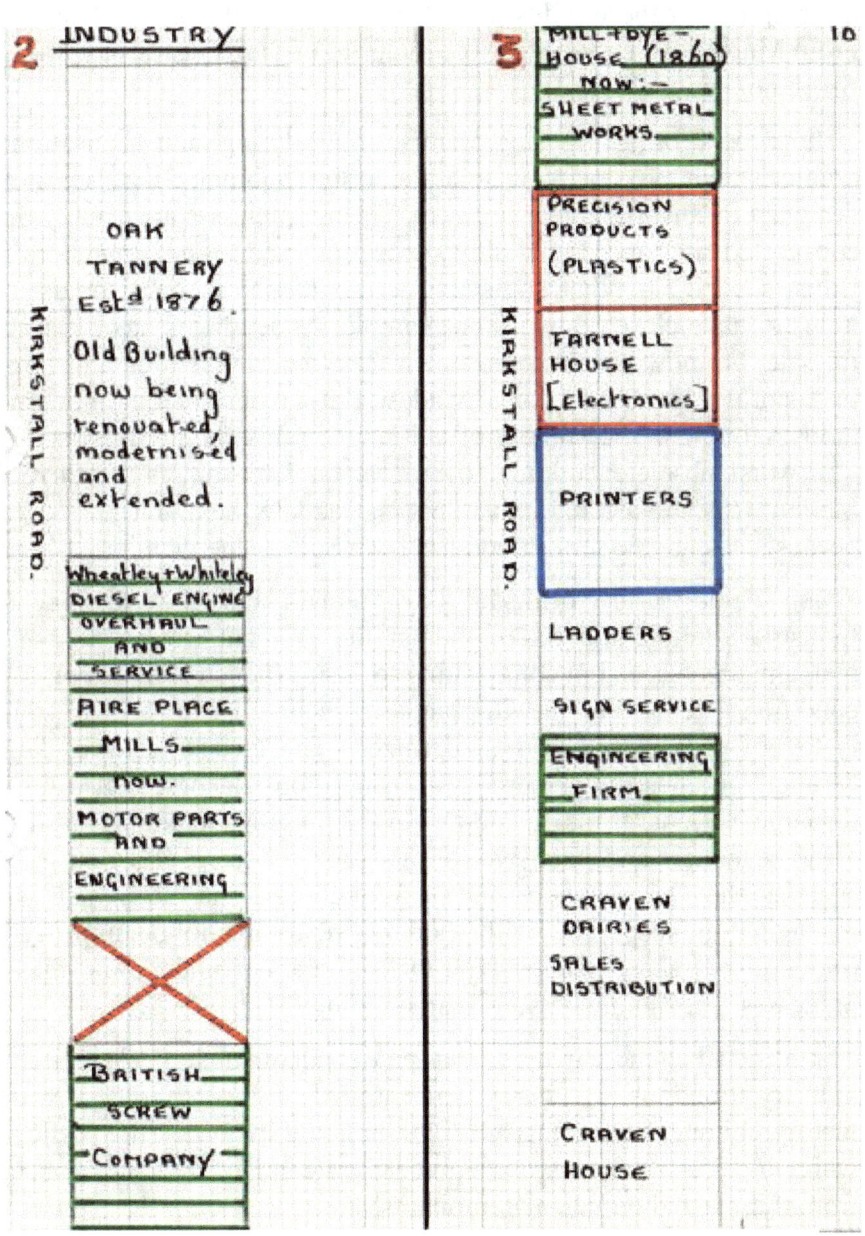

Map 10

As can be gathered from the Maps 9 to 11, where dates are supplied, the majority of these industries are old, well established industries. From Map 15 we can see that the majority of the industries are local firms, not national ones.

These local forms are using premises built during industrialisation; premises that are today unsuitable, often buildings that are not designed for that particular industry. The old premises are usually on constricted sites and do not allow space for expansion. A number of firms, see Fig. 15. that could not cope with the modern trends in industry have closed down. For example, Abbey Mills has been up for sale, but now it has closed down. The building is long and low, two storeys high, with tiny windows; it is obsolete in modern, industrial terms. The number of buildings in this condition is rising. The worst obsolete building to be seen in Kirkstall, is the Power Station. It is so vast and ugly. This is gradually being closed down because a clean, modern station has been built in the vicinity.

Map 7 shows how Kirkstall is to remain a part of the Leeds Industrial Belt in the future, but at the moment it is just about managing to succeed in contributing to Leeds Industry. In its present condition its contribution will gradually decline. However, Kirkstall is to be re-developed and modernized. The closed factories and derelict buildings are all marked for demolition. The new Belt will be for large National firms, in contrast to the present situation. The sites are to be modern and extensive, allowing for extension. Old industries such as the Oak Tannery and J. Woodhouse and Sons that are managing to keep pace with modern trends are to be improved (modernised) and extended. The Oak Tannery is undergoing these processes at the moment, so it is an ongoing trend.

In the new belt there will be an emphasis put on modern, clean, light industry. Previously, industry concentrated on heavy industry with factory chimneys churning out fog and smog over the Aire Valley, which in 1950-1960 caused a high death rate in Kirkstall and Burley, from asthma and bronchial complaints.

At the moment only a small part of the vast changes planned for

Kirkstall's industry have been completed. This is a large scale industrial development sited on an area that five years ago provided dense back to back working class housing for the workers in the local Kirkstall factories.

This new industrial development is situated between Kirkstall and Burley - see Maps 12 and 13. As can be seen, it will be an area made up of light industries. Yorkshire Television Studios are also planned for this area (opened in 1968), plus a bowling Alley and entertainment area.

The main reason why Kirkstall is to be a Light Industrial Belt while the South and South East Belts will concentrate on heavy industry, is because of its proximity to residential areas especially Burley; so only clean industries are to be developed. The idea is similar to the one adopted in the New Towns, where industry is being put into an industrial belt separated from the residential areas by an amenity open space of grassland, see Map 14 and for a complete picture in 1981 see Map27. Kirkstall and Burley Road are to be improved as they will be important distributor roads. Light industries will rely on road transport rather than the River Aire and Leeds and Liverpool Canal and railway. From Maps 7, 14 and 27 we can grasp what Kirkstall's light industrial belt will be like in 1981, but at the moment, the planners are at demolition stage. They are at the first stage of demolishing the back to back houses around the existing factories; these have been due for demolition since 1949. Next, some of the factories will be demolished, only then can light industry development take place. Industrial development is always slow and because this area is so old and in need of a complete renewal, the development may take longer than normal.

Kirkstall in the future will have a concise, purely industrial belt and suburb concentrating on light industry.

4. Industry in Kirkstall Road.

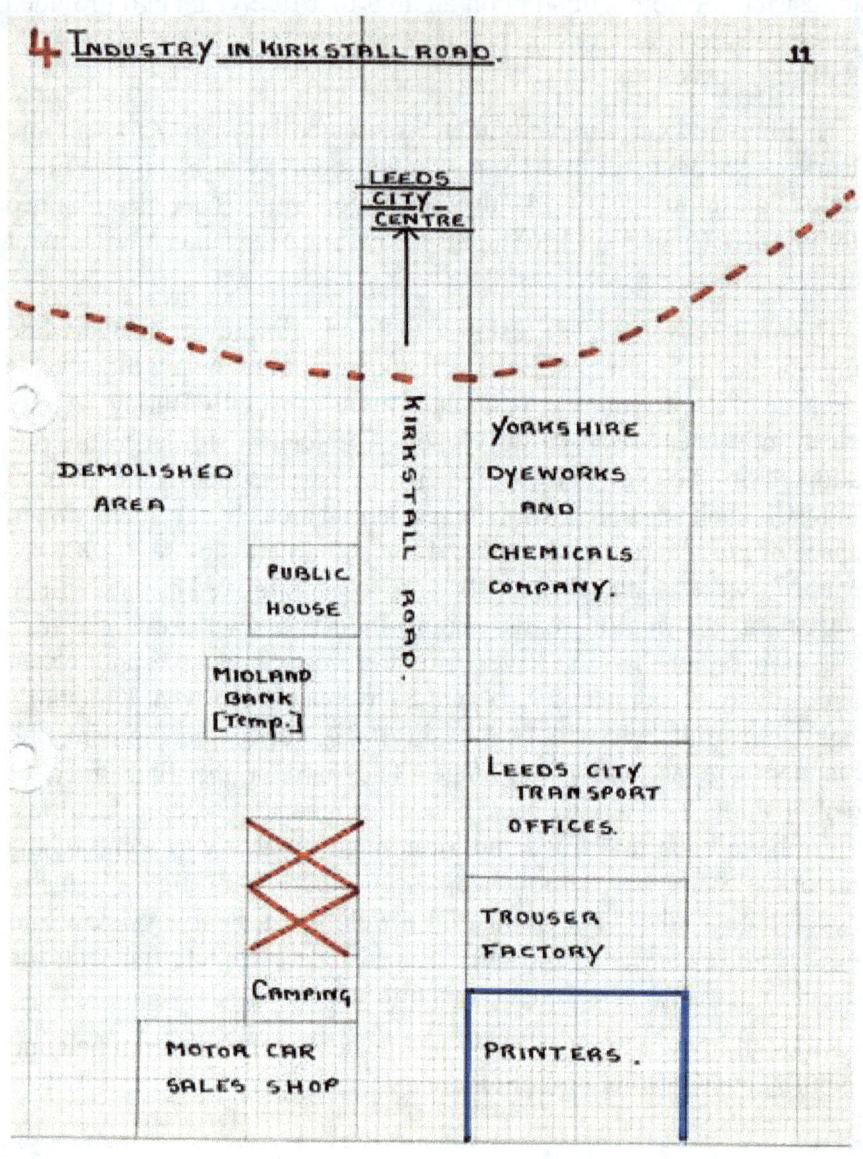

Map 11

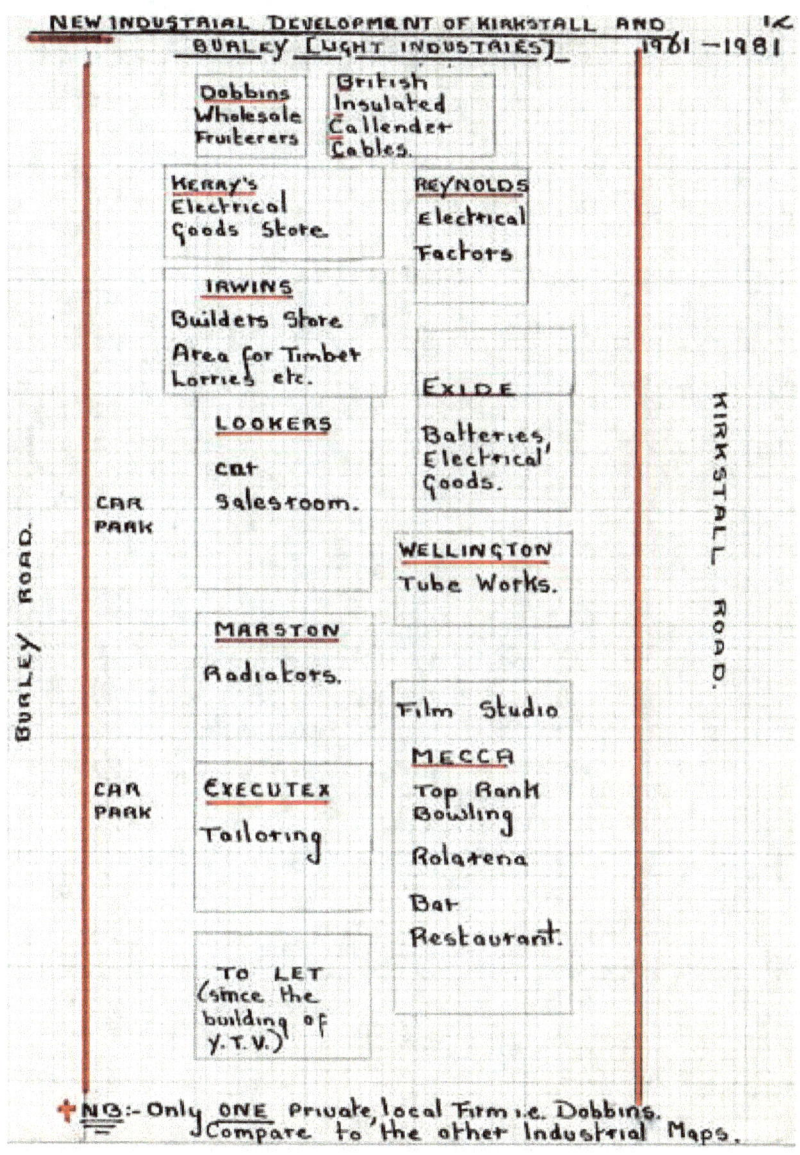

Map 12

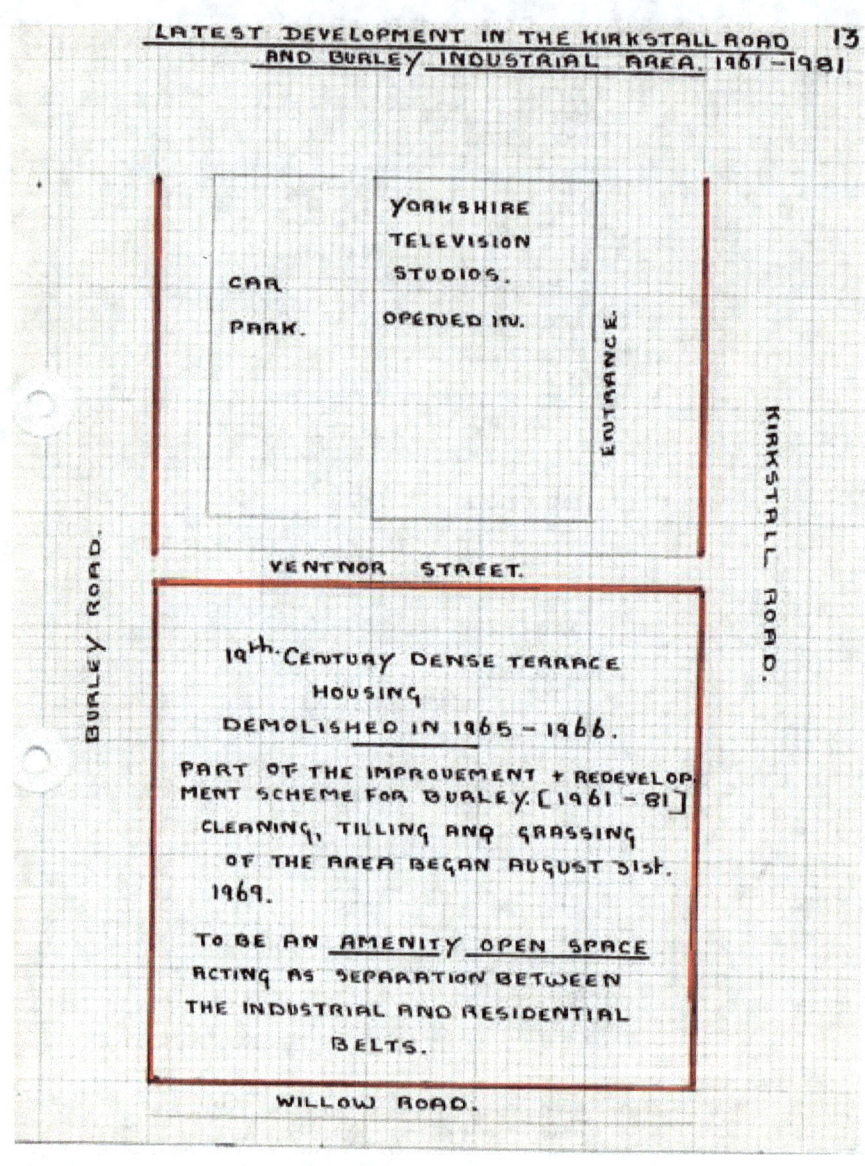

Map 13

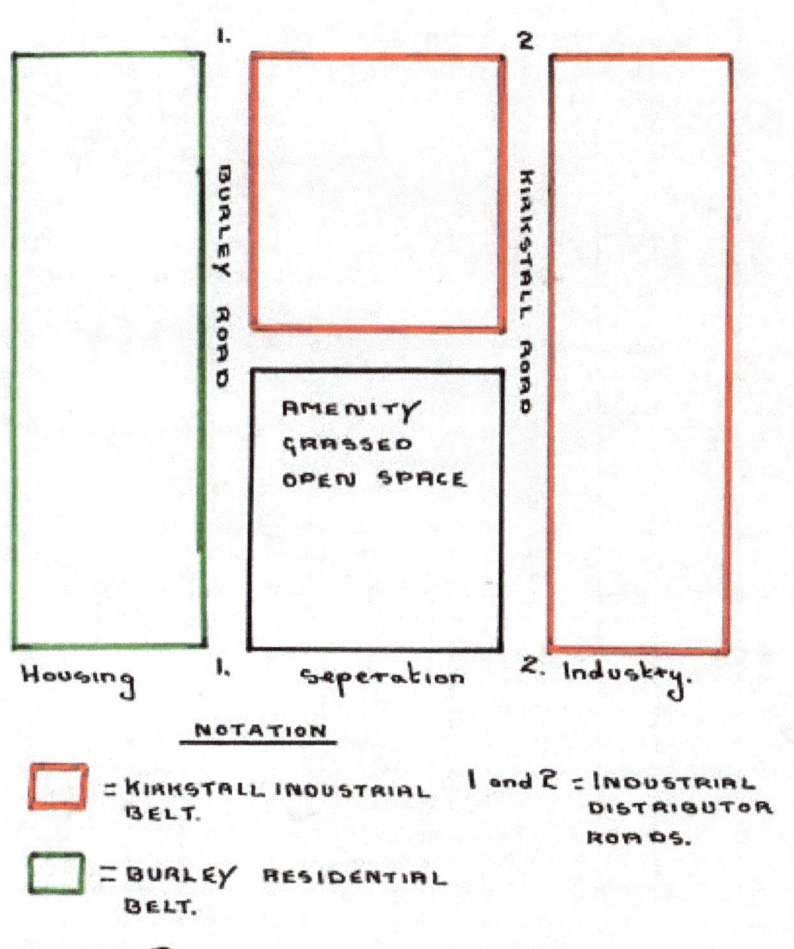

Map 14

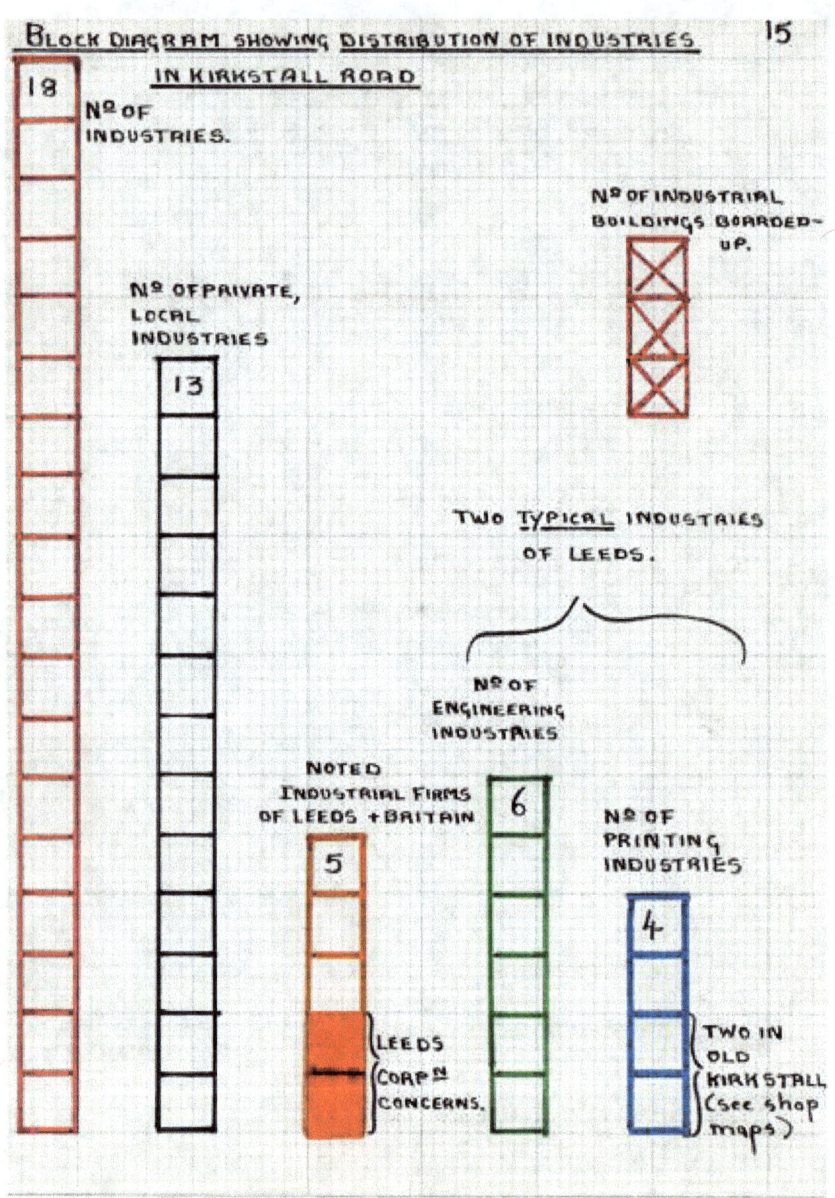

Map 15

Industry in Woodhouse can be located at the junction of Woodhouse Street and Meanwood Road. Most of the information about the industry in this area can be gained from Map 16.

There are a variety of types of industry which again typify Leeds Industry. The emphasis, if any, being on iron and metal work. Meanwood is more overspills of this industry, although Woodhouse Clothing Company is in derelict premises, and it is only a small firm. Two old industries, see Maps 30 and 33, in the shopping area, are now closed down. In the past, one was a timber and timber goods firm and the other a wholesale clothing factory. These are now due for demolition, as indeed much of this area is. Woodhouse is the oldest suburb or the first to be urbanized and is now in a poor state. However, rapid development is taking place which will be dealt with in the chapters on housing and shopping. Woodhouse will cease to have any industry; it will be a completely residential suburb as it was originally. It will extend parallel to Meanwood Industrial belt which is to be modernized and re-developed in the same manner as Kirkstall.

At present we can still categorise Woodhouse as an industrial suburb because of its few remaining industries and especially for its dense, pattern of back to back houses, but in the future Woodhouse will be a purely residential area probably providing housing for workers in the city centre such as secretaries, shop assistants and so on.

As regard to Burley there are one or two small, private well established "factories" or businesses, but nothing of significance. There is one industry in Headingley Hill however which should be mentioned. Indeed, it is in fact more of a research area than an industry. It is the W. I. R. A. that is the Wool Industries Research Association. When the Yorkshire College of Science was established a cloth-workers company became interested in opening a Textile department. This was the origin of Leeds University and its Textile Department. When Textile Sciences became more and more important, the W. I. R. A. was created. It does studies and research into the strength, suitability and mending of worsted cloth, providing valuable information for woollen factories. It has also invented machinery and devices for the improving of the efficiency of the woollen industry in general. For details, see next page.

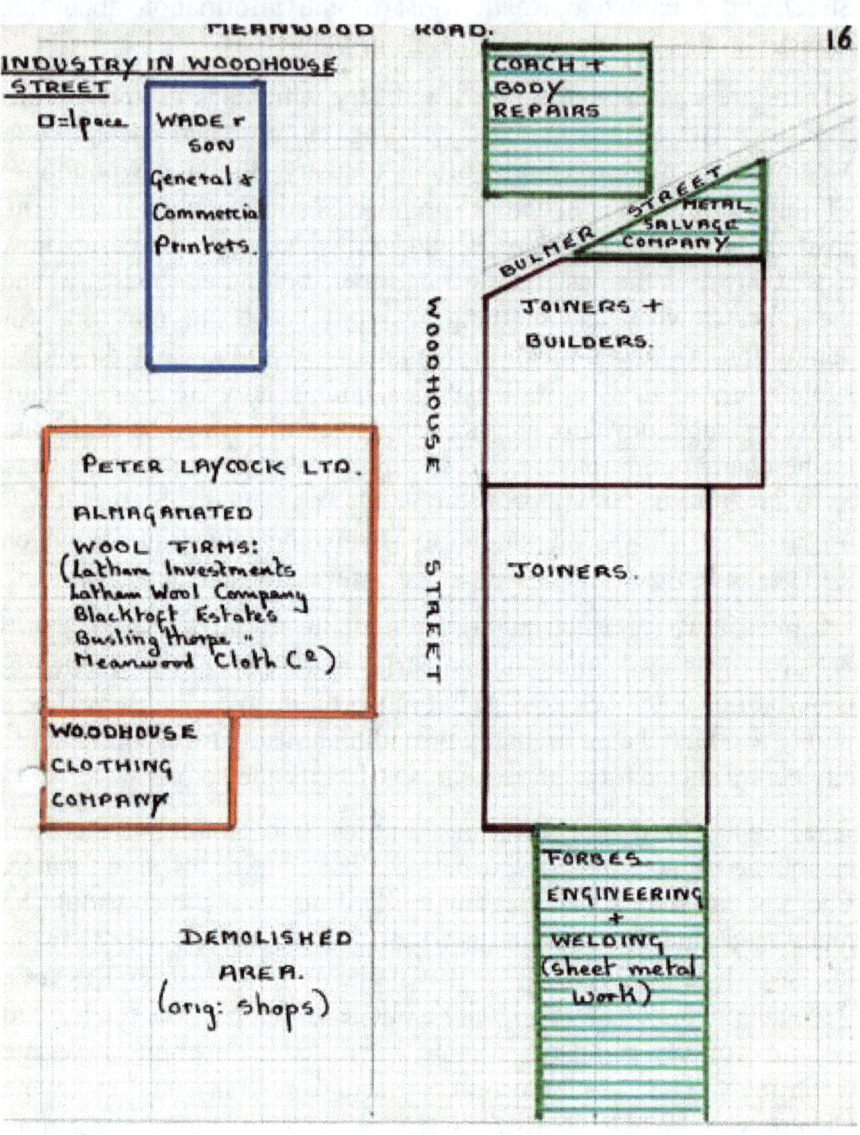

Map 16

The W. I. R. A.

The W. I. R. A. is an organisation with a staff of 200 people. It was formed in 1918, in Leeds city centre, but later they bought a house in Headingley called "Torridon's" which was adapted into laboratories. The W. I. R. A. is locally referred to as "Torridon's" today. Much modernisation has been done recently and extensions have been added in the last few years. It is a thriving entity. Early research involved the physical and chemical constitution of wool. The moisture content in wool, its molecular make-up in relation to the various treatments (i.e., shrink-resist) applied to the fabrics.

W. I. R. A. won the Nobel Prize Award in 1952. The machinery it invented include:

- W. I. R. A. Autocount: It is an automatic method of controlling the slubbing process in woollen carding
- W. I. R. A. Full-width Temple: for eliminating increases in warp tension, thus reducing yarn breaks and the suchlike.
- The detailed study of the Mending of worsted cloth has been an important achievement.
- Testing Devices:
- W. I. R. A. Fibre Fineness Meter: for speedy measurement by an airflow of the diameter of a sample of fibres.
- W. I. R. A. Fibre Diagram Machine. For measuring and presenting graphically the distribution of fibre length.
- Rapid Drying Oven: bringing one pound (1lb) sample fibres from normal moisture content to dry weight in five minutes.
- W. I. R. A. Automatic Recording Balance: for weighing and recording samples.

An instrument for measuring the extension and tension breaking load of single fibres. The last three of the mentioned inventions are fairly recent devices (1966) and were entered into the International Exhibition. The above gives us some indication of the amount of study and research done at W. I. R. A.

Yorkshire Dyeware and Chemical Company

See Industry Map 11. In Britain, the main centres for the manufacture of dyestuffs are Manchester and Huddersfield, which are both conveniently situated close to the Yorkshire Textile area which is the largest user of their output.

However, one important dyestuffs firm is located in Leeds, precisely in Kirkstall's industrial belt. This is the Yorkshire Dyeware and Chemical Company. It was formed in 1900 by the amalgamation of several small firms dealing in natural dyewoods and extracts.

It has expanded rapidly in recent years and now there are two factories, manufacturing a wide range of synthetic dyes. It is best known for its extensive range of disperse dyes which the company has developed during the past thirty years. Disperse dyes are a type essential for colouring many man-made fibres especially cellulose acetate and polyester fibres. One natural dye is still in use and still important. It is logwood.

Colour chemistry and dyeing in Leeds has become widely known because of the Leeds University Department. The formation of this department of Dyeing is again due to the company of cloth workers who in 1875 set up the Department of Textiles.

Chapter 5: Urbanisation

In Chapter Two we saw that the differentiation of the suburbs lay in the type of urbanization that had taken place. We also saw the type of housing to be found in Kirkstall for example and how it contrasted with the housing pattern in Headingley.

It is necessary to study this period of Urban Growth more closely in order to understand its bearing on the present housing situation and standards in the four suburbs.

Urban Growth began in the 19th Century, a mushroom growth in the early 1900s, then later the built up areas spread along the radial road system. This was the pattern followed in Kirkstall, Woodhouse and later Headingley. Housing gradually spread across the intervening districts. In our case, this was the small suburb of Burley.

Growth of Leeds suburbs was more concentrated on the North side of the city, that is in our area of study: Kirkstall, Woodhouse, Burley and Headingley.

Rapid industrialisation in the 19th Century meant that housing was urgently needed for the workers. A large number of houses had to be built and quickly; they also had to be close to the factories, so houses of a poor quality were erected. Back to back houses were built, mingling with the factories; up to eighty to ninety back to backs were built per acre.

In Leeds before 1844, 30,000 back to backs were built. Between 1844 and 1874, another 28,000 went up and another 12,000 by 1909. In the study area, back to back housing was found in Woodhouse and Kirkstall and also in that part of Burley which adjoined Kirkstall.

In Kirkstall and Woodhouse, the pattern was for dense housing with rows upon rows of back to backs opposite the industries as can be seen in the growth rings in Map 6

Parts of Burley adopted the same building plan. Remaining parts of Burley nearer to Headingley, had houses of a slightly higher standard, although it was still Corporation Terrace Housing. The better class residential areas were built on higher ground as far away from the smog and dirt as possible, away from the central area of congestion and overcrowding. Headingley falls into this category of suburb.

Housing was not urgently needed in Headingley. It was owned by the wealthy so the City Corporation could not take it for their housing purposes. Housing development was done privately and selectively by the rich owners. In the 19th Century the houses in Headingly were large, single family houses, often detached villas in their own grounds owned by bankers, industrialists, and the like.

When the urbanized areas began to get overcrowded and too dense and people began to spread out and extend the town's limit, Headingley became more populated. This phenomenon was known as "sub urbanization" and took place in the 1900s. (see Map 6). In order to meet this need, Leeds Corporation began to build terraced houses and semi-detached houses. The further out of Headingley one travelled, towards Adel, the better the houses were.

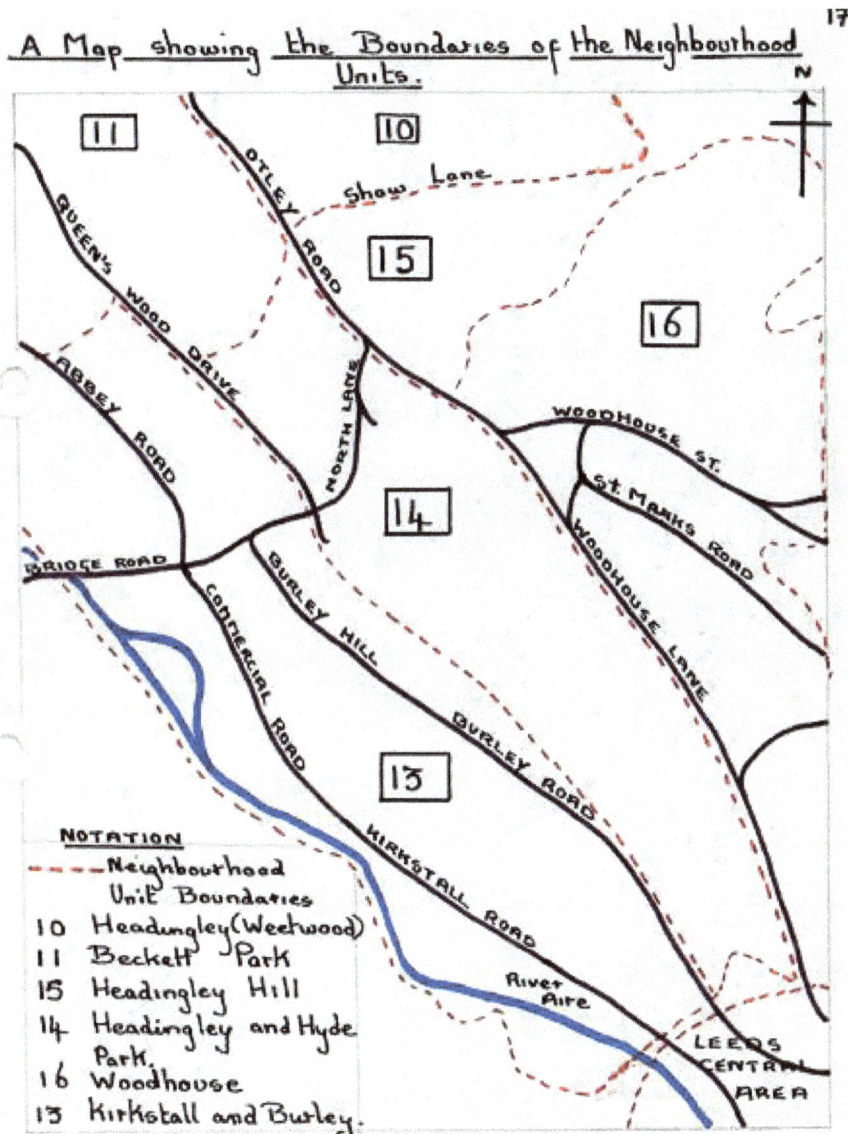

Map 17

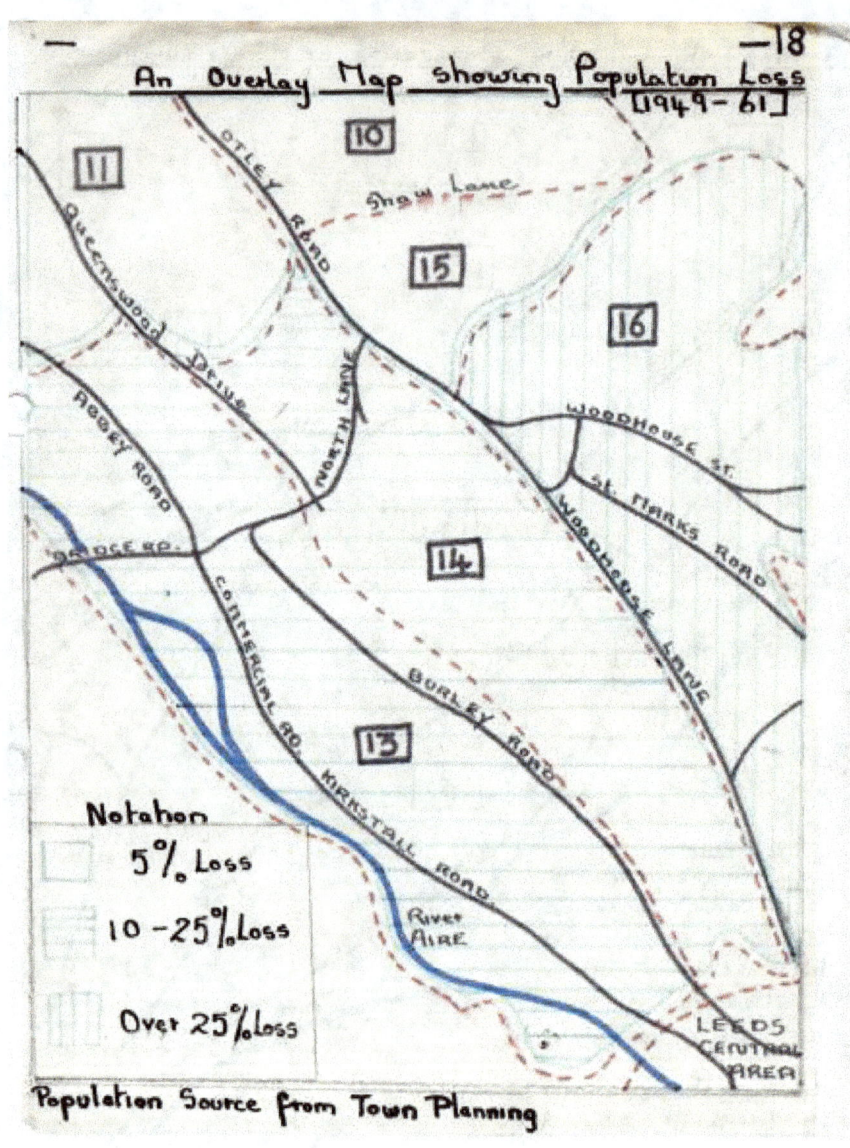

Map 18

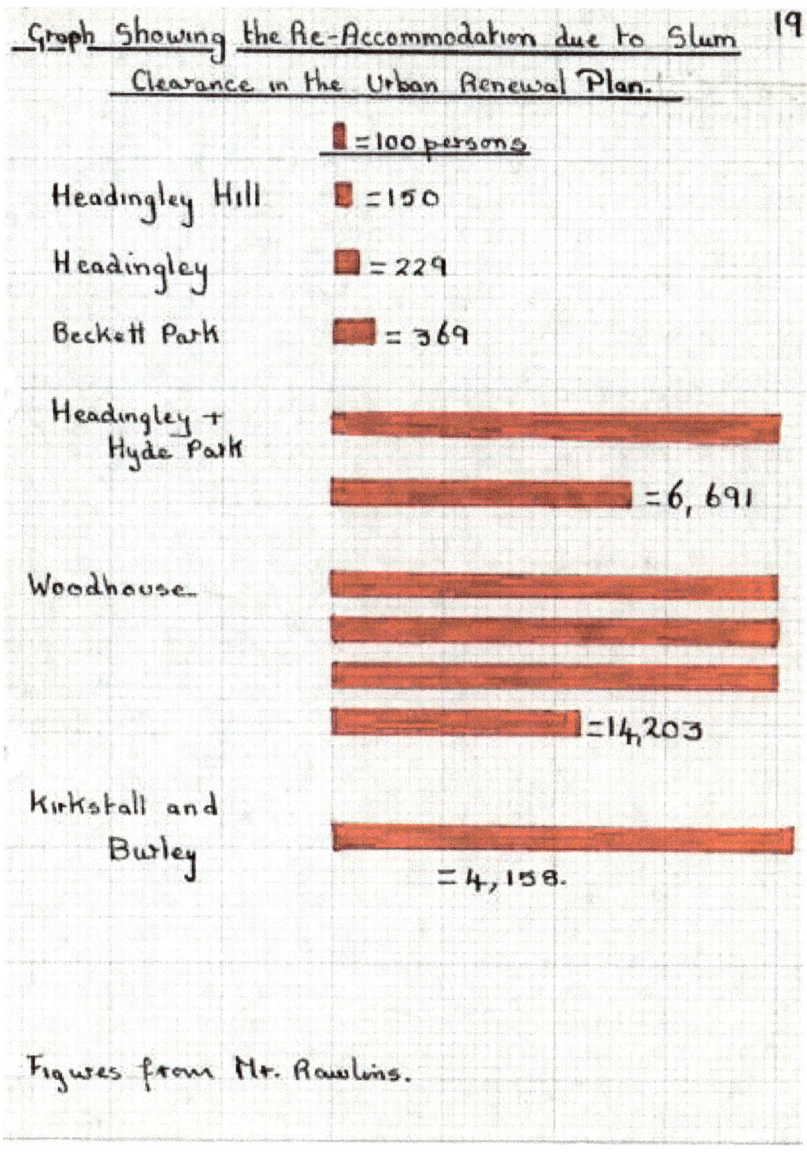

Map 19

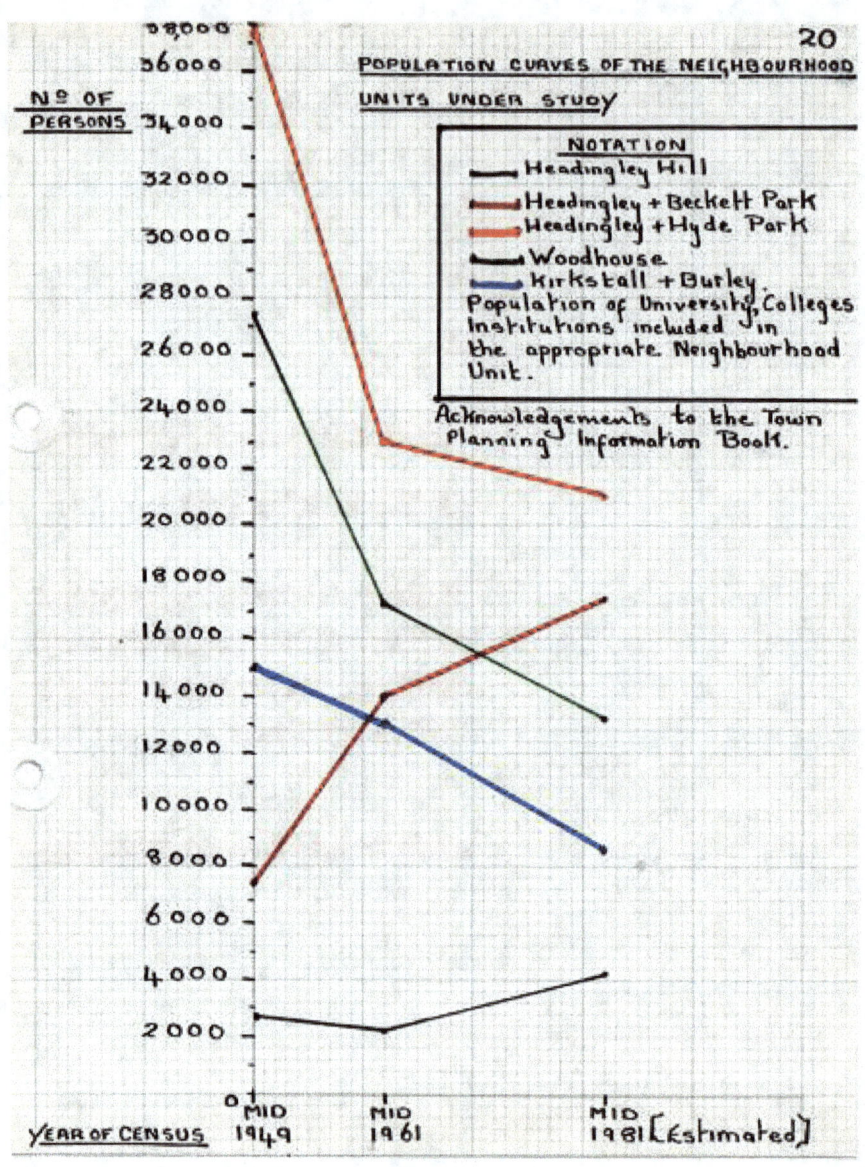

Map 20

Chart giving Population Figures of Neighbourhood Units under Study

Neighbourhood Unit (suburb)	Unit Nº	MID 1949	MID 1961	MID 1981 [Estimated]
Headingley Hill	15	2,700	2,500	4,300
Headingley and Beckett Park † (Housing Estate)	10 / 11	4,100 / 3,600	3,700 / 10,300	5,100 / 12,300
Headingley and Hyde Park	14	37,600	22,900	21,000
Woodhouse †	16	27,700	17,400	13,400
Kirkstall and Burley	13	15,000	13,000	8,600

† = University, Colleges etc. included in Population Figures.

Acknowledgements to Town Planning

Map 21

Chapter 6: Slum Clearance

By 1930 Kirkstall, Burley, Woodhouse and Headingley were densely built up areas. From 1933 to 1934 Leeds City Council planned to demolish 30,000 of the poor quality back-to-back houses. By 1939, 14,000 had been cleared. Then came the Second World War.

After the War in 1949. The Government and Local Authorities had a great deal of work regarding the housing situation in the country. In Kirkstall, Burley, Woodhouse and Headingley not much damage had been done during the War, but the houses were old and in poor condition, having been neglected over the war period. Leeds City Council issued a Housing Development Plan for 1949 to 1961 to deal with these shabby areas.

As we shall see, slum clearance went ahead at quite a rapid speed, but they had by no means cleared the suburbs of all the slums. Besides, due to the financial situation of the country – the so-called aftermath of the war – new housing was not built or the number of houses to be built was reduced.

Dissatisfied with this situation, in 1960 Leeds City Council made a review of the 1949 to 1961 Development Plan, for the 1961 to 1981 period. Concerning housing, the first aim was to get rid of all the slums that had been waiting for demolition since 1949. The rate of slum clearance was speeded up; in the whole of Leeds in 1962 8,500 slums were demolished and they were cleared at a rate of 2,300 per year. By 1966 the slum clearance programme had been completed.

Map 18 shows that between 1949 and 1961 all four of the suburbs suffered a loss of population which indicates a movement of people and also slum clearance. Within the last twenty years there has been a strong movement of the population within the city boundaries. Slum clearance meant re-housing of many people who settled in the new, more pleasant suburbs of Leeds, such as Seacroft, for example. There has been a movement outward, away from the crowded, congested city areas toward new, very suburban housing estates. Shifts of population are important for the siting of industry and service industries but also for transport and communication facilities.

Map 18 shows that Woodhouse is the suburb that suffered the worst loss of population, of over 25%, which shows how great a slum clearance must have taken place. The larger part of the 260 acres of Woodhouse was cleared of its old housing and Map 19 shows the number of persons re-accommodated due to slum clearance. We can see how Woodhouse lost 14,203 people.

Headingley and Hyde Park, Kirkstall and Burley lost 10 to 25% of its population which together meant re-accommodation of nearly 2,000 people. Most of these people moved to the newer housing estates on the outskirts of Leeds.

From Population Map 20 and supplied figures in Map 21 we can see the drop in population in all four suburbs by mid-1961. The population figures were high in 1949 especially for Headingley and Hyde Park, yet by 1961 the population curves had declined quite steeply (except in the cases of Headingley Hill and Far Headingley).

In 1949, Headingley and Hyde Park had a population of 37,600, yet by mid-1961 it had fallen to 22,000 due to slum clearance and the general shift to the new suburban areas.

Those suburbs in Map 20 that are declining in population and therefore in population density will continue to decline up to 1981 despite urban renewal and development. By 1981 the population density will be in complete contrast to the high density of Industrial times. Kirkstall and Burley will move from 13,000 to 8,600 inhabitants which corresponds with the plan making Kirkstall primarily an Industrial Belt.

Headingley Hill and Headingley in Map 18 show that their population has remained fairly static, having a slight loss of 5 %. Although Map 19 predicts re-accommodation figures after slum clearance in Headingley Hill and Headingley, I have not been aware of any clearance. However, there has been a great deal of slum clearance in the Beckett Park area, which is considered to be part of the Headingley Unit. In the 1950s and 1960s, Beckett Park housing consisted of a series of Army huts and a mass of small bungalow "prefabs" extending up Queenswood Drive. These were built as emergency homes for the un-housed Leeds population after the Second World War and they were still inhabited in 1965. They were demolished in 1966 and the new Beckett Park housing estate extends up Queenswood Drive into West Park, see overlay on Map 26.

From Map 19, 369 people from the Beckett Park slum area had to be re-housed and naturally they were re-housed on this new estate, also many people from the Woodhouse slum area came to Beckett Park to live which meant that from 1949 to present day (1966) over 7,000 houses have been built on this estate - see relevant part in Fig. 21. The housing is typical of present day (1966) council housing estates with semi-detached houses. At the lower end of the estate there are a series of multi-storey flats.

From the maps we have seen a decline and loss of population in these suburbs. The suburb units remain the same in acreage, so naturally one can assume a decline in population density. However, from Map 22, which shows an estimated population density for 1961 to 1981, we foresee a rise in the density. Indeed, the population density is higher today in Headingley than in any other of the three suburbs. It has 30 people per acre but by 1981 each will have risen by 10 people per acre.

From one source on the population maps we have established that the population is on the decline, yet this density estimate for 1961 to 1981 indicates there will be a rise in population. I can offer no explanation at this point for this variance in data, except that there may be some commuting into some suburbs which raises the population figures. This could be possible in Kirkstall due to industry and also because of the rise of businesses in Headingley. This remains only a theory and anyway we are only dealing with estimates.

Since 1961 to 1968 the rate of slum clearance in Kirkstall, Woodhouse and Beckett Park has been tremendous. Within this seven-year period, slum clearance has far surpassed development.

Although, in some areas, such as Beckett Park, clearance and redevelopment have taken place alongside each other – showing development can be rapid when better standard housing is required urgently.

This chapter on slum clearance includes a large part of my study area but we should also take a glance at the situation where housing in bad condition still exists, and demolition is not taking place. Also, what are the plans for the future of the suburbs that have been partially demolished? This question leads us into the following chapter.

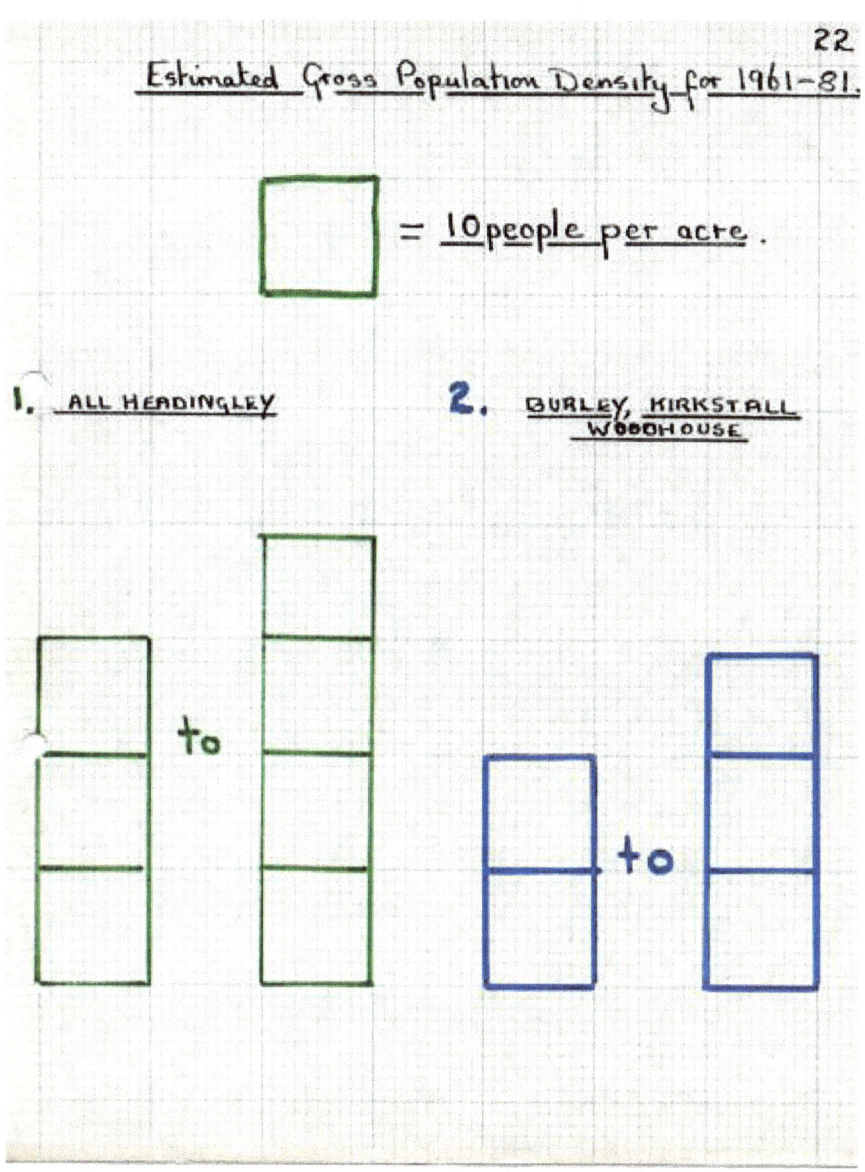

Map 22

Chapter 7: Urban Renewal and Development

In the previous chapter we had a look at population figures in relation to slum clearance (Map 24). Now we must look to the next part in the cycle, which is renewal and developments. This period is referred to as Urban Renewal and Rehabilitation.

Kirkstall, Burley, Woodhouse and Headingley were given a great deal of attention in the 1961-1981 Plan, because they are such old suburbs. Development and re-development were planned to give each suburb a definite role to play in the city.

With regard to the houses remaining in Kirkstall, Burley, Woodhouse and Headingley, they were not of a poor standard enough to be considered slums nor modern enough to be adequate for contemporary standards. They are referred to as Twilight Housing. Map 23 shows the boundary of the older housing; this area is known as the Twilight Zone which includes all of the four suburbs, except for Far Headingley.

Before we can look at the renewal of the suburbs, we must extract the problems hindering their development, especially in Woodhouse, Burley and Kirkstall. Problem is maybe the wrong word, because it is the people living in these three suburbs who could prevent them from becoming suburbs with a better standard of living and a more pleasant environment.

Kirkstall, Burley and Woodhouse housing is the oldest and most shabby; the more wealthy people moved out of these areas to new corporation estates, leaving these houses in a state of decline. For this reason, they were relatively cheap in price. These houses were gradually overtaken by the large poorer families; families where the father was less skilled and earning very little to support a large family of four or five children. A fair proportion of families who settled in these areas were Irish.

At the same time, Leeds University had been expanding rapidly over this period and its intake of students had increased accordingly. The University itself was just not able to cope with housing the large influx of new undergraduates. The trend was for students to rent flats or whole houses out of university control. Many of these students rented these poorer houses for their accommodation especially those in the proximity of the University campus which are Burley and Woodhouse.

A Map showing the zone of Older Housing in Leeds.

NOTATION
- — — — City Boundary
- ——— Boundary of Old Housing
- ▭ Study Area
- 🟧 City Central Area.

SCALE: 0 1 2 3 miles

Acknowledgements to Town Planning Information.

Map 23

Householding [1961]

Neighbourhood	Nº of Private Householders	Type of Housing
Far Headingley	8,517	Post 1930. Mainly Private Development.
Hyde Park	5,754	Dense Victorian Terrace Housing — overcrowding.
Kirkstall	6,480	Older Back to Back Terrace Housing. Some recent Corporation Housing.
Woodhouse	6,528	Dense Terrace Housing

Housing Development

Year	Original Housing Plan	Completed Housing
1949–1956	12,000	16,139
1956–1961	11,340	15,013
	23,340	31,152

Figures and Information from the Town Planning Book. C.G. Thirlwall C.B.E. M.Eng.

Map 24

With the bulge of immigrants in those years, there was an urgent need for housing. They were, as matter of course, given the older housing properties which could accommodate large families and were also suitable for their purses. They usually wanted to settle together in a community, close to their family and friends. Relatives and friends of the same family were frequently housed in one house to spread the cost. This is still happening today in Woodhouse, Kirkstall and Burley. Quite a large community of Pakistanis have settled in Burley, for example. As more of the old houses are being emptied, they are being quickly overtaken by the Pakistanis and so their community grows.

Therefore, in Kirkstall, Burley and Woodhouse we have a population mainly of these types: the large poorer families, students, and immigrants. Those remaining are old people who are well settled in their homes because they have always lived there. The houses here are already in a sad state of decline and inadequate by modern standards but these types of people mentioned above, for various reasons, are types of community that take little care of their environment, so these areas are sinking more and more into decline. From Map 25 and Image 25 we have evidence of the results of living in a poor environment, in Burley.

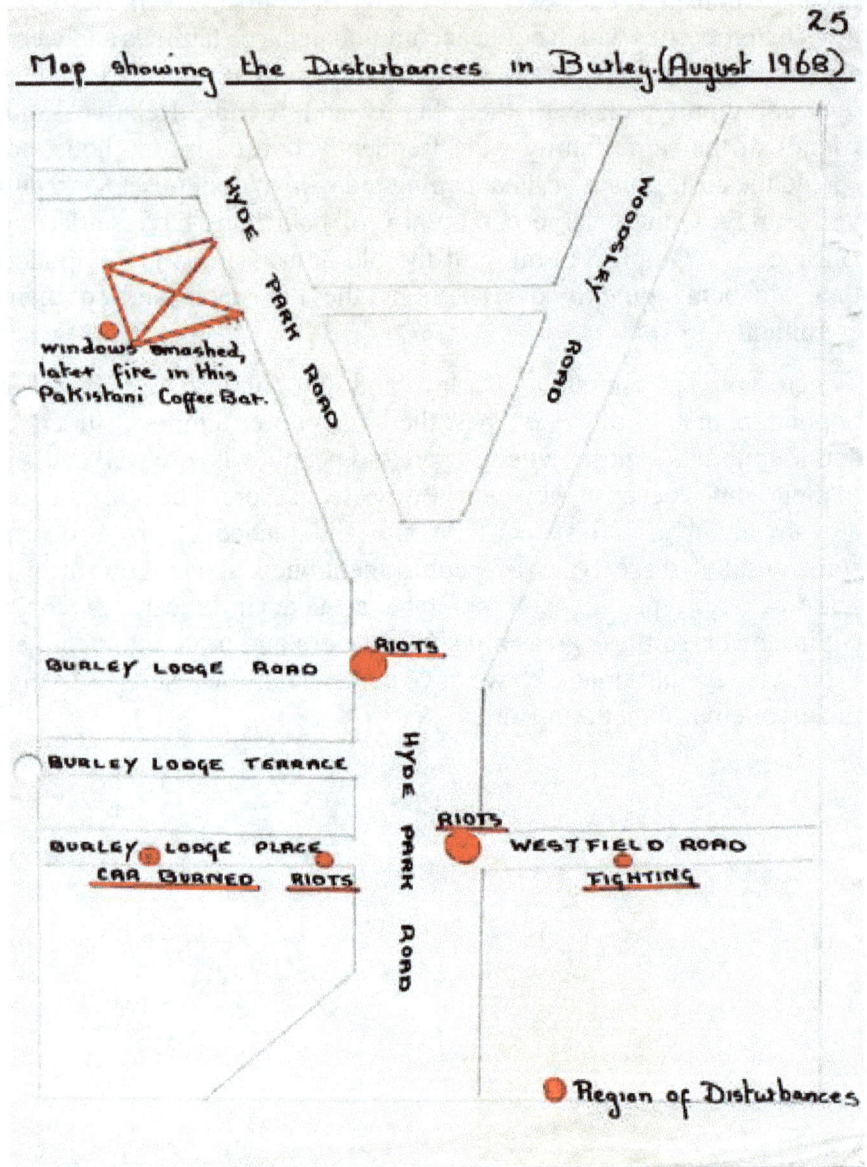

Map 25

The newspaper cuttings show there were clashes between the large poor families and the immigrants which took place in August 1969. It was nothing too serious, but it had supposedly stemmed from racial intolerance. However, most of the trouble decidedly originated from the poor living conditions and dissatisfaction with the environment in which they lived.

Immediately following these disturbances, redevelopment began - see Map 26. The blue horizontal lines mark the Burley Redevelopment area.

Re-development is not taking place in the whole suburb of Burley but just in the older parts, which are the ones nearest the city centre area and the housing opposite Kirkstall's industries.

Re-development stops at Burley Park, which forms a green belt boundary, separating the old part from the newer, more northerly part.

The old housing is of the dense, terraced type with narrow back streets and a great deal of back-to-back houses, which are still occupied in Burley by immigrants and large poorer families. They have no gardens and there are no public gardens in the vicinity; the nearest "green" area is Burley Park.

Many of Burley's back-to-back houses were demolished in 1965, an area which now forms the present site of the New Light Industrial Area of Kirkstall and Burley. See Map 13. Some of the land was left open to become an Amenity open space area for Burley but it was not until the trouble broke out that this land was cleared of rubbish and tipping of the previous four years. On August $31^{st,}$ this open space was finally tilled and grassed which makes a vast improvement to the area. Burley is gradually being re developed but a lot of the big old houses still remain and still in a bad condition, yet I have been unable to find any information about future plans for them.

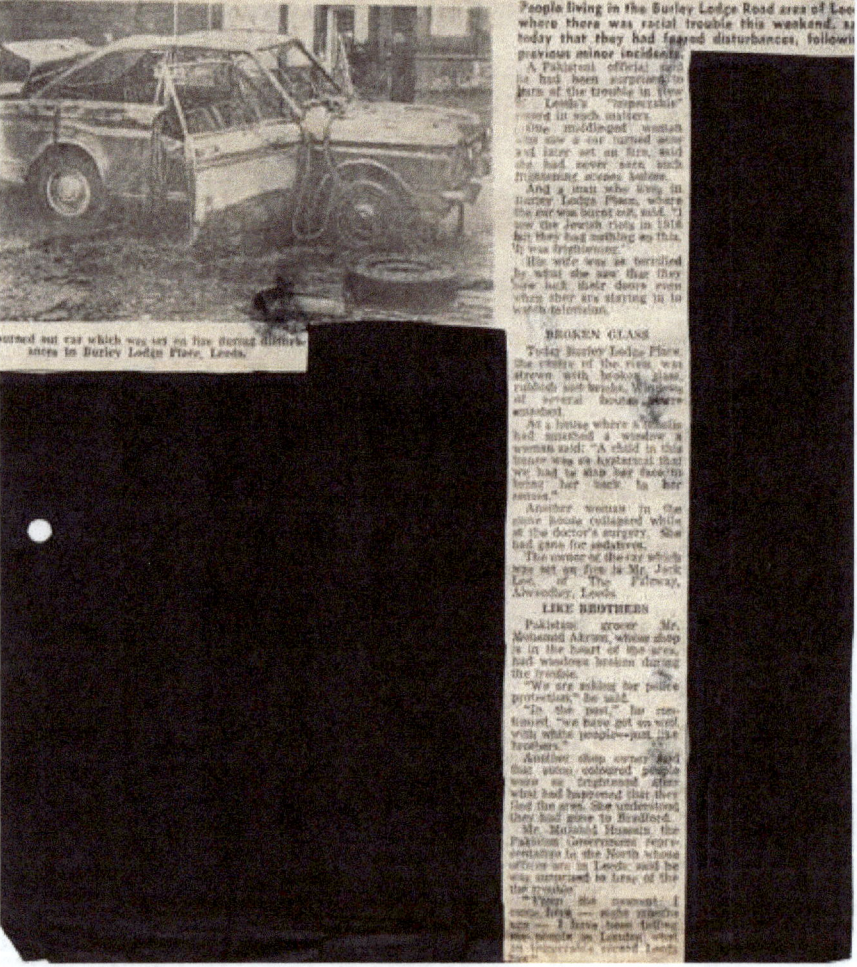

Figure 25

Figure 25B

And in a not-so-happy area

'Stay in' plea at trouble-spot

Following further anti-immigrant disturbances in the Barley Lodge Road area of Leeds, appeals were made today by an immigrant organisation and a worker for racial equality for coloured immigrants to stay indoors at night.

Flashpoint in last night's trouble came when a crowd of 500 people converged at the corner of Woodsley Road near the junctions of Barley Lodge Road and Westfield Road.

Today Mr. P. G. J. Shah, chairman of the Pakistan-Muslim Association in Leeds, urged all coloured people to stay indoors at night until the trouble dies down.

"We have advised them to stay inside and not to create any trouble by going out while there is all this trouble," he said.

PERSONAL PLEA

A close watch was being kept on the area by the Yorkshire Conciliation Committee of the Race Relations Board, and Mrs. Maureen Baker, secretary of the Congress of Racial Equality, has made a personal plea to immigrants not to go around in large groups, leaving their women and children at home at night.

She has had several calls from immigrants expressing anxiety over the recent trouble.

"Some were rather puzzled as to why it had happened and others said they would be prepared to leave the district," she said.

WRONG, SHE SAYS

Mrs. Baker said it would be wrong if the immigrants were forced out of the area.

An appeal to the citizens of Leeds to maintain racial harmony, "one of the cherished traditions of the city," was made today by Indian immigrant organisations in Leeds—the Sikh Temple, the Indian Workers Association, and the Ramgarhia Board of Leeds, an immigrant social welfare society.

"The trouble last night started after rising time at public houses and lasted for over an hour.

After cries of "Get the Pakis", "Go Home Wogs" and the throwing of "We Shall Not Be Moved" there were scuffles with the police.

Suddenly, the crowd moved into Hyde Park Road and congregated outside the cafe and grocer's shop

12 arrests say police

A Leeds City Police spokesman said today: "As a result of incidents of disorder last night in the Leeds 6 area—Barley Road strictly—12 people were arrested and charged with offences under the Public Order Act 1936.

"Two windows were broken but no one was injured. The people will be appearing in court next Tuesday, August 2, when the 23 other similar people, arrested the previous night, will also be appearing."

Figure 25C

There is no indication of modernization of the terraced houses or plans to give them a "new look" which is the current trend.

Re-development will consist of Burley becoming a non-traffic area. Burley will be a quiet, completely residential suburb, presumably, the existing houses will fit in around new, small squares lined with trees, small grass areas and seating. Alterations have now begun. However, this does not solve the housing situation, the over-tenancy of greedy landlords and overcrowding with immigrants and students. It does raise the standards of the suburb a little, compared to previously. Perhaps the planners have decided that improvements to such a dense housing area would be a waste of public money, because the houses will be ready for demolition within the next ten years. Meanwhile they are "patching up" Burley, making the environment more pleasant, which they define as re-development.

The standard of living in Burley is quite low if one judges from its external appearance. The houses are good solid houses, but they are dirty and in need of paint. Many of them have outside "privies" or toilets, some houses do not have bathrooms. Windows are dirty or broken. Washing is hung on washing lines stretched across the streets and litter is strewn in the gutters. Burley Park is the only green area in this densely populated area. It is a large expanse of grassland with a recreational play area. tennis courts, a bowling green and a Children's Nursery.

As can be seen from Map 26 and by now it is evident that a large part of Kirkstall is planned to be demolished. We know of re-development in Burley and the new large housing estate planned for the Beckett Park area to house the inhabitants from these areas, so Kirkstall will eventually be solely industrial. However, at the moment most of Kirkstall is still at the demolition stage and a large number of houses still remain to be cleared. In the overlay on Map 26 we can see the amount of demolition completed in relation to what is still to be cleared. Demolition is not straight forward; it requires weaving around the factories. When demolition is eventually completed, the cleared areas will have made the way for new factories and depots, the so called light industries, which will be small in ground coverage with three or four storeys.

Extending North West out of Kirkstall, along Kirkstall Road and away from the Industrial Belt, Leeds Corporation has built a series of multi-storey flats in this same area, but on lower ground. Many bungalows have been built by the Corporation for the Welfare Committee, providing homes for the aged. This new unit of housing was completed in the latter years of 1960s. See the overlay of Map 26 – area 4.

The housing situation in Headingley is different compared to the other areas because housing developed later and more selectively, so the condition of the houses is not as bad as other areas. At the moment, the housing situation in Headingley is static – none have been demolished and none have been built. Most of the houses in Headingley are large, created for large families with maybe a servant or two, but too large for the average sized family of today, so more and more of these houses are being converted into flats, mostly for students at the nearby University and college, especially the nearby Beckett Park College of Education and Carnegie Hall (a sports college). The previously high standard of living in this better class suburb is slowly being spoilt by this type of student flat life and the new role given to the area. It has brought a lower standard of living.

At the time of writing Headingley is still a busy, prosperous suburb, but over time it has lost some of its higher tones. However, Headingley now has a new function which will prevent it from declining in the same way as its neighbouring suburbs. The fact that Headingley is becoming a large district shopping area, serving a wide area stretching as far out as the edge of Leeds boundaries will ensure a prosperous future.

Much has already been said about the immense slum clearance in Woodhouse. Now it is actually in the position of being one third completely cleared, one third built or re-built and one third open land. When so much housing has to be cleared it is inevitable that the clearance rate will outpass the development rate, but people are pleased to be rid of the back to back eyesores. Now they have to look at weed strewn open spaces until development can begin.

One area in particular in Woodhouse, has been cleared, between St. Marks Road and Woodhouse Street - see Map26. New housing was rapidly developed, in the form of high rise flats. A whole series of multi–storey flats have been erected amid surrounding untilled land and on-going demolition. It is a time of transition.

Moving into that part of Woodhouse which meets Meanwood and the city central area, known as Camp Road, another mass of multi-storey flats have been built, again surrounded by open, untilled land. Vast open spaces remain empty, awaiting development. A large number of people are still waiting to be accommodated in new housing which still has to be built.

At present there are only two relatively small areas with new housing. Development rate is slow, even though there is so much availability of land. Woodhouse will eventually provide homes for 18,000 people, new schools, churches and shopping facilities. Woodhouse has almost been totally demolished. It is actually undergoing complete urban renewal and will become a modern, purely residential suburb. It has an extensive development scheme which will take many years to complete.

The Educational Precinct

Apart from the large re-development scheme for Woodhouse, regarding new housing, shopping areas and such, Woodhouse also contains a large part of the Leeds Educational Precinct.

The Yorkshire College of Science was established in 1874 and the purpose of the college was "to supply instruction in the Sciences which are applicable to the manufacturers, engineering works, mining and agricultural sectors of the County of York". In due course it became one of the constituent colleges of the Federal Victoria University. Finally, in 1904, it received is own charter and so we have the beginning of Leeds University.

In the beginning of the 20th Century Leeds was the centre of industry, it had always been traditionally industrial, and they could see no need for developing Leeds education. However, in the last twenty years (1949 – 1969) there has been emphasis put on building for educational purposes to overcome the inadequate provision for Further education in all spheres but especially technical education.

From Map 26 we see the extent of the University Precinct. The map shows the area in blue. It clearly shows the extent of the Central Colleges, the Inner Ring Road for Leeds, and the new multi-storey flats areas. These lay originally in the suburb of Woodhouse in the part known as Little Woodhouse and Carlton Hill. These were the better class areas of Woodhouse but because they were the nearest to the City Centre and the centre needed to expand its limits, this area had to be completely demolished. The area was demolished in 1964 and development began immediately afterwards.

The University began to expand rapidly in 1960 with the introduction of the Chamberlain Plan which made the University and the Leeds Infirmary into one complete unit. Development was planned for a 7,000-student body. In 1965 the number was increased to 9,000 and new plans say the student population will soon become 10, 000.

The University departments in their original parts are housed in the large houses and villas built in industrial times when Woodhouse was a wealthy suburb. The Lydden Estate owned by Mrs Lydden was sold off to the University when Woodhouse started to lose its residential, suburban qualities to the working populations. The Lydden estate is now part of the University Campus and streets in the area are named after her. But today, major development is planned for the University campus: the University-Hospital is planned. The University has already expanded with several new buildings and halls of Residence, planned in such a way that it links with the Hospital extending into Leeds City Centre with a no–traffic / all pedestrian area.

The once clear boundary between Leeds Central area and Woodhouse has become somewhat blurred. A similar situation has occurred with the Central Colleges; they were built on the site that was a part of the Woodhouse suburb but as development progressed this part was given over to the new Central area and although an actual boundary line does not exist between the two, it is as if Woodhouse has been absorbed. The building of these Central colleges is still in progress; they are being opened and put to use immediately, as soon as they are completed. Three colleges are being built: the College of Technology, the College of Commerce, and the College of Art, all sharing a central library. There are plans for another five colleges of various subjects. These colleges already exist and are housed in the large, old buildings scattered over Leeds. Eventually they are going to be brought together in one educational campus, known as the Leeds Polytechnic.

In Map 27 we have a made–up plan of what the study area should look like when all the developments mentioned in this chapter have finally been completed, by 1981. There is a vast residential area in red made up of Burley, Woodhouse and Headingley suburbs. The Educational Precinct, that is the University-Hospital and Central Colleges will have merged into one, linking with the City centre and Civic Centre (A+ B). The green belt marks the beginning of the industrial belt of Kirkstall. Map 27 indicates the future urban, industrial, and educational structure and future appearance of the four suburbs under study.

House clearance and amount of re-development

NOTATION TO MAP 26

Amount of House Clearance and Re-development
MAP: Housing Clearance 1949 - 1981

    Housing Clearance {1949 - 1961} / {1961 - 1981}

    Re-development Area (Burley)

    University Precinct.

1. Woodhouse Moor
2. Headingley Cricket Ground.
3. Burley Park
4. Beckett Park
5. Kirkstall Abbey + Grounds.

OVERLAY: Areas cleared at Present (1969)

    Areas where House Clearance is Completed, or in Progress.

    Clearance and Re-development.

1. The Leeds Polytechnic (Central Colleges)
2. Kirkstall/Burley Light Industry.
3. Part of the Inner Ring Road + Multi Storey Car Park.
4. Kirkstall Welfare Housing + Flats.
5. Car Park and Car Wash.

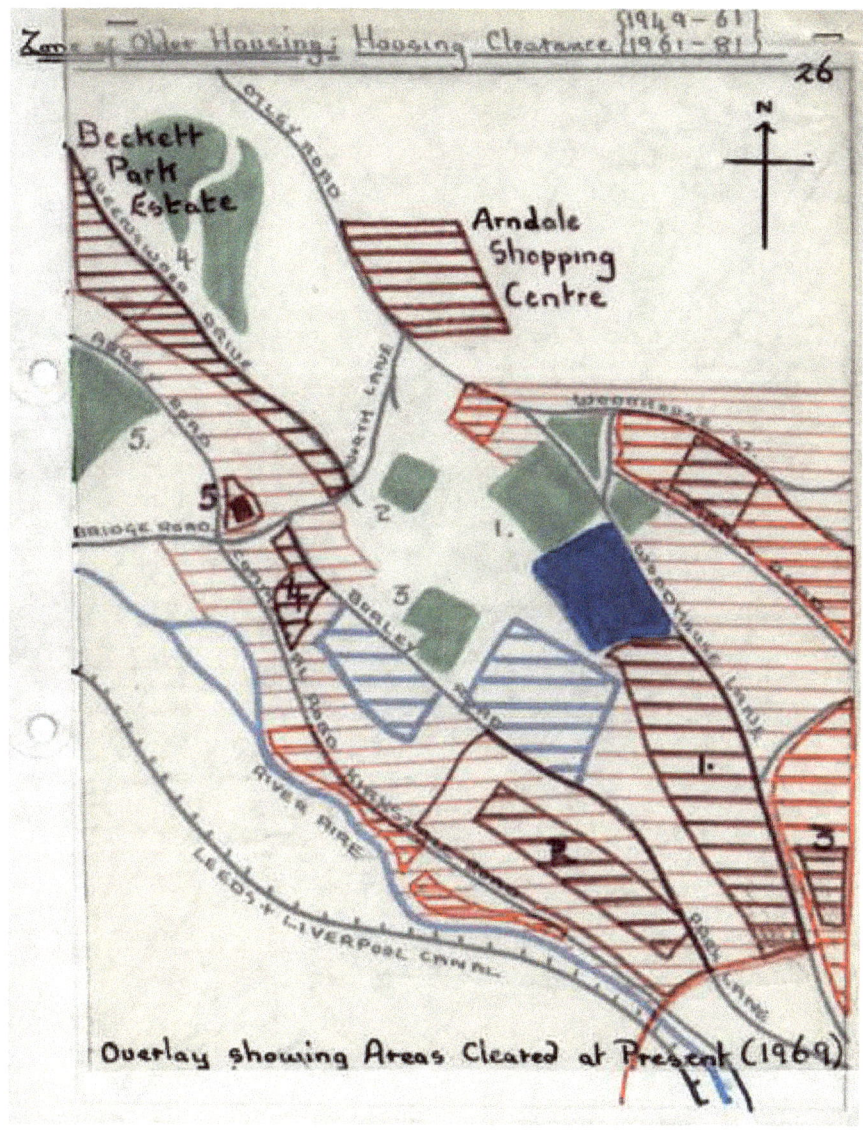

Map 26

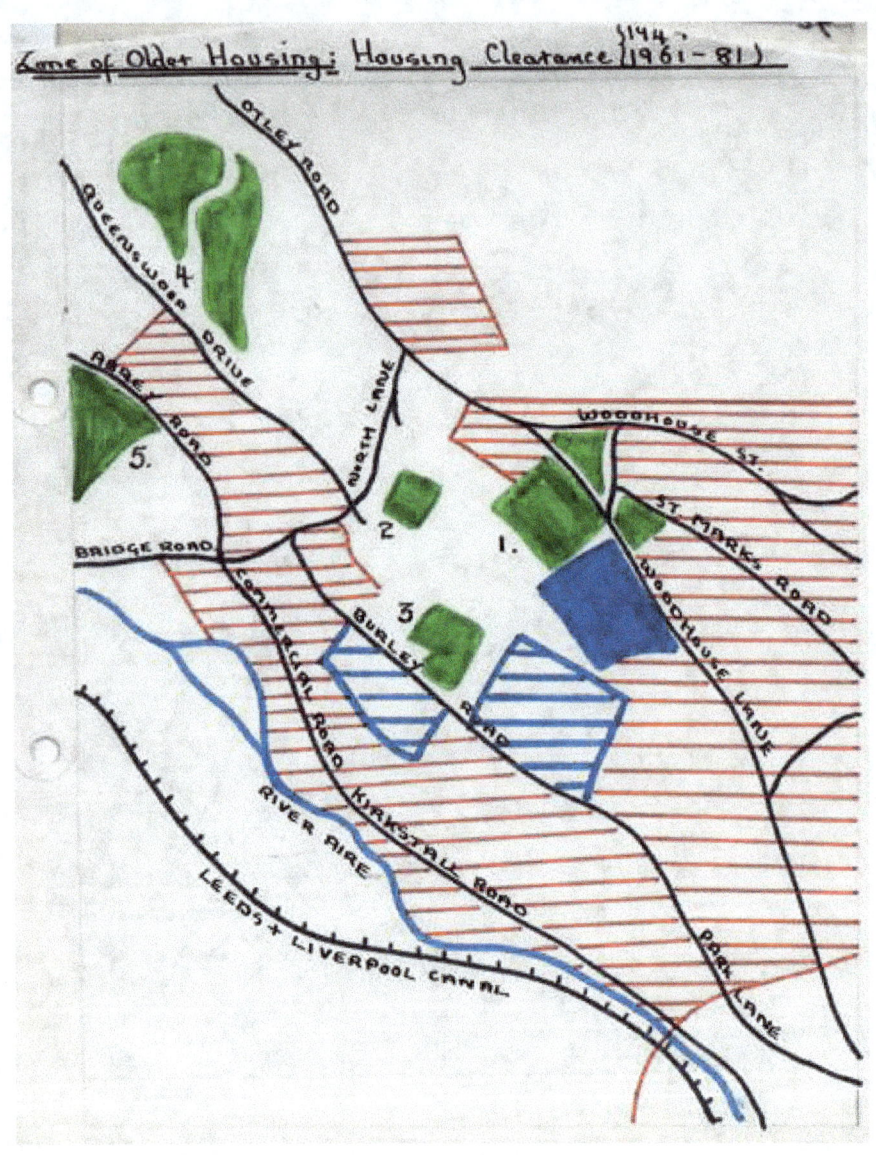

Map 26 overlay

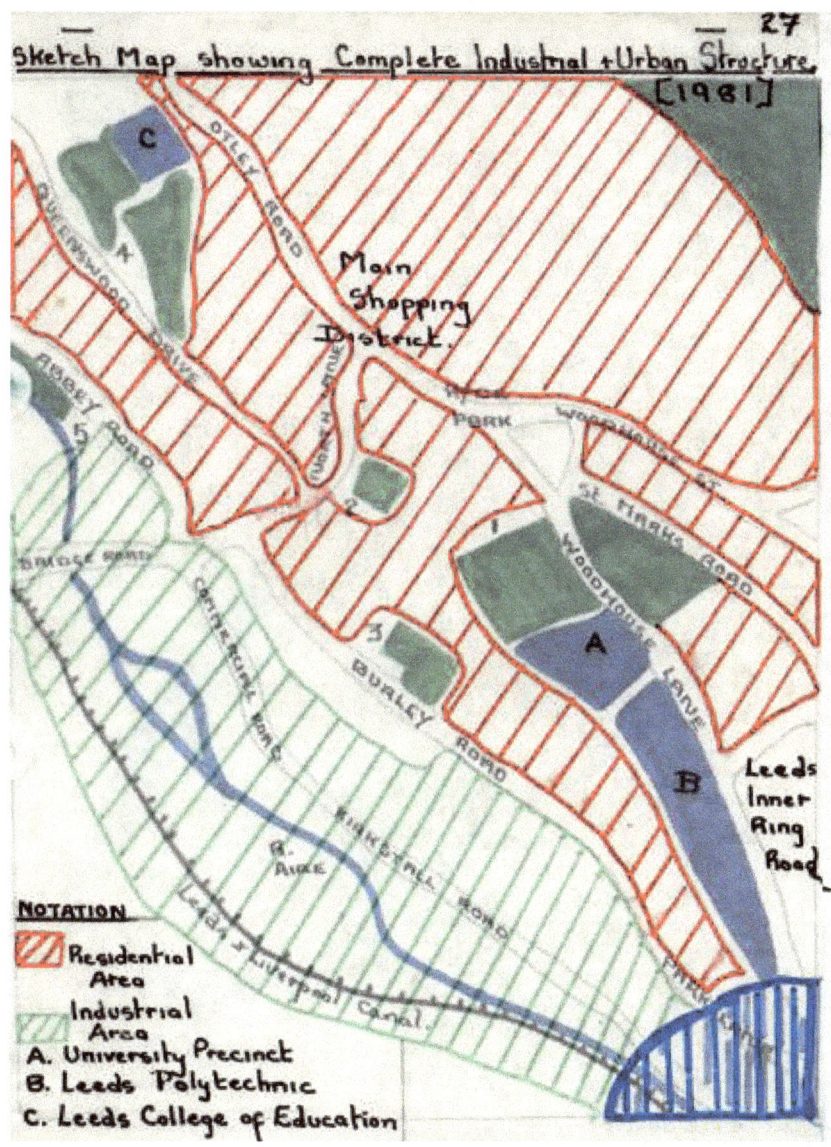

Map 27

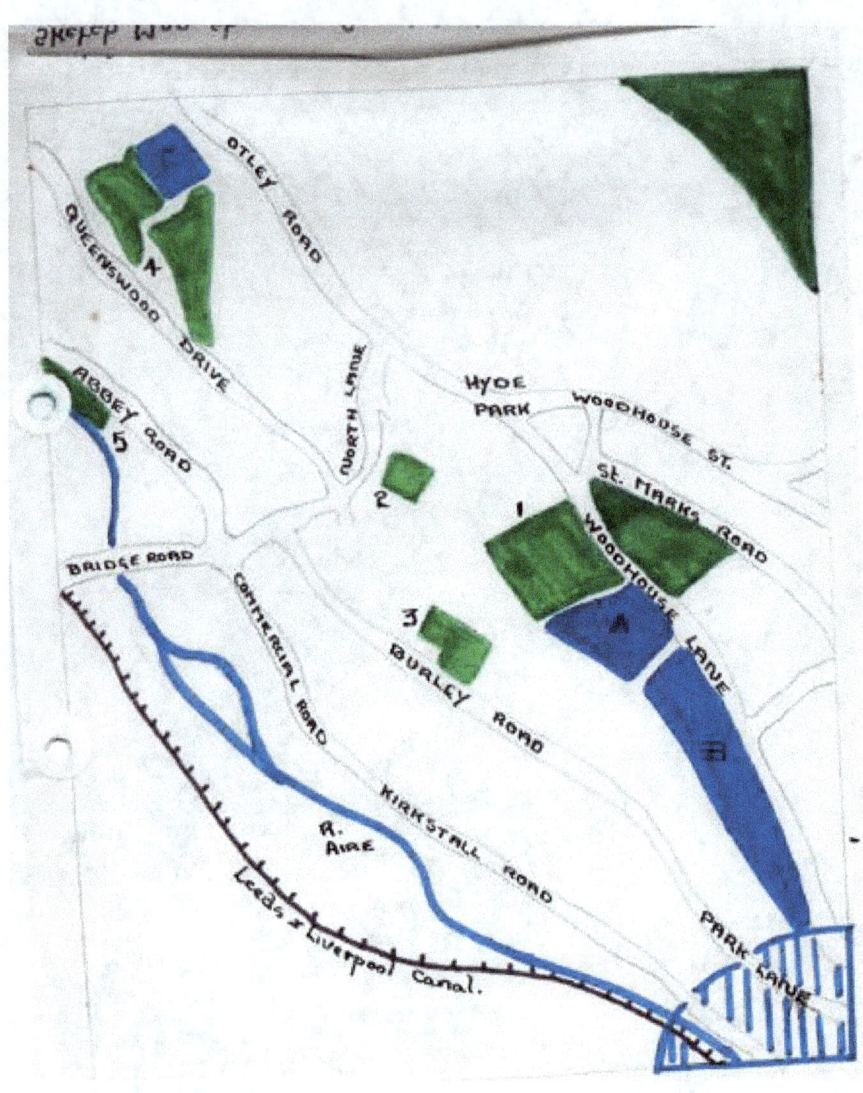

Map 27 overlay

Chapter 8: The Shopping Facilities

In the past each suburb had been designed to be self-sufficient, each containing its own necessary shops, churches, and transport, all within easy reach of the residential part. Each suburb had its own shopping area but then a fashion developed of shops being built at the end of the rows of houses, on the corner of the street, as shown below.

These small corner shops developed to serve the immediate local area, offering everyday products that people often ran out of such as salt or sugar, whilst the main bulk of shopping was done in the main shopping areas.

In Headingley, for example, there was one main shopping area but four smaller "local" groups of shops within the suburb. This shopping pattern was popular in the 1800s and many examples of it still exist today, for example in Woodhouse – see Map 31 and also in Kirkstall - see Map 35, 36 and 38. However, in some parts of Kirkstall, where slum clearance has started, a lot of these shops have now been boarded up, ready for demolition. The back-to-back houses next to these shops are also awaiting demolition or are in the process of being demolished, as I write.

Another pattern, which is still evident today, was to build the shops all the same size, small and in a long continuous row down the main street, called a parade of shops, which became known as the High Street of the suburb.

NOTATION TO SHOPS

AGE OF SHOPS:-

☐ (orange outline)   NEW SHOPS (1967-1968)

☐ (blue outline)   UNDER 20 YEAR OLD SHOPS

☐ (green outline)   OLD SHOPS (DATED + UNDATED)

☒ (orange, with X)   SHOPS NOW BOARDED-UP.

☐ "TO LET" (dashed)   SHOPS TO LET

☐ (green outline with orange side)   OLD SHOPS WITH A NEW FRONT.

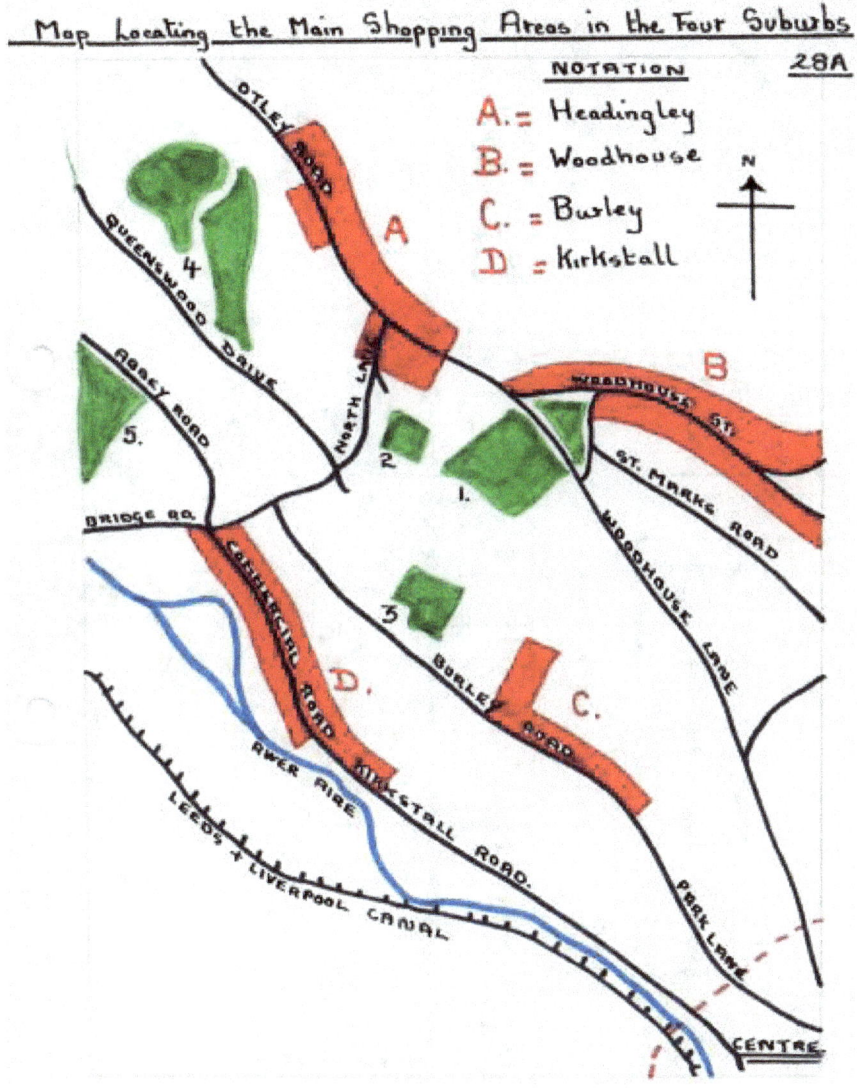

Map 28

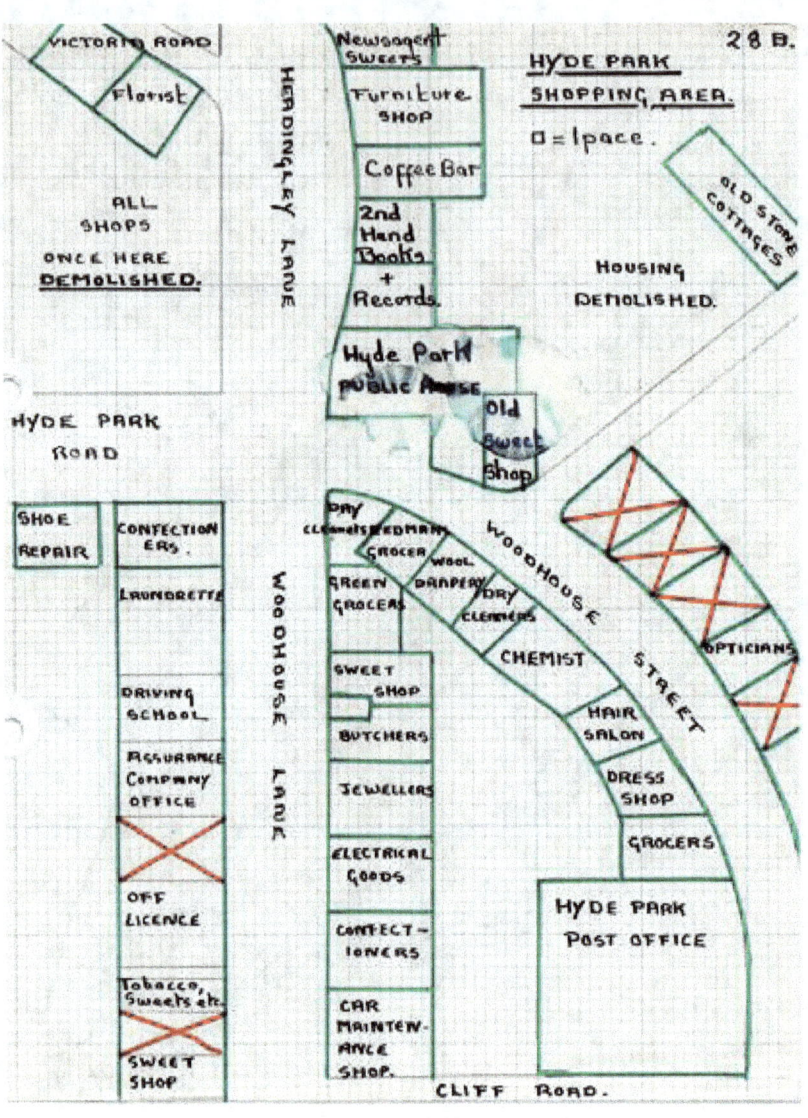

Map 28B

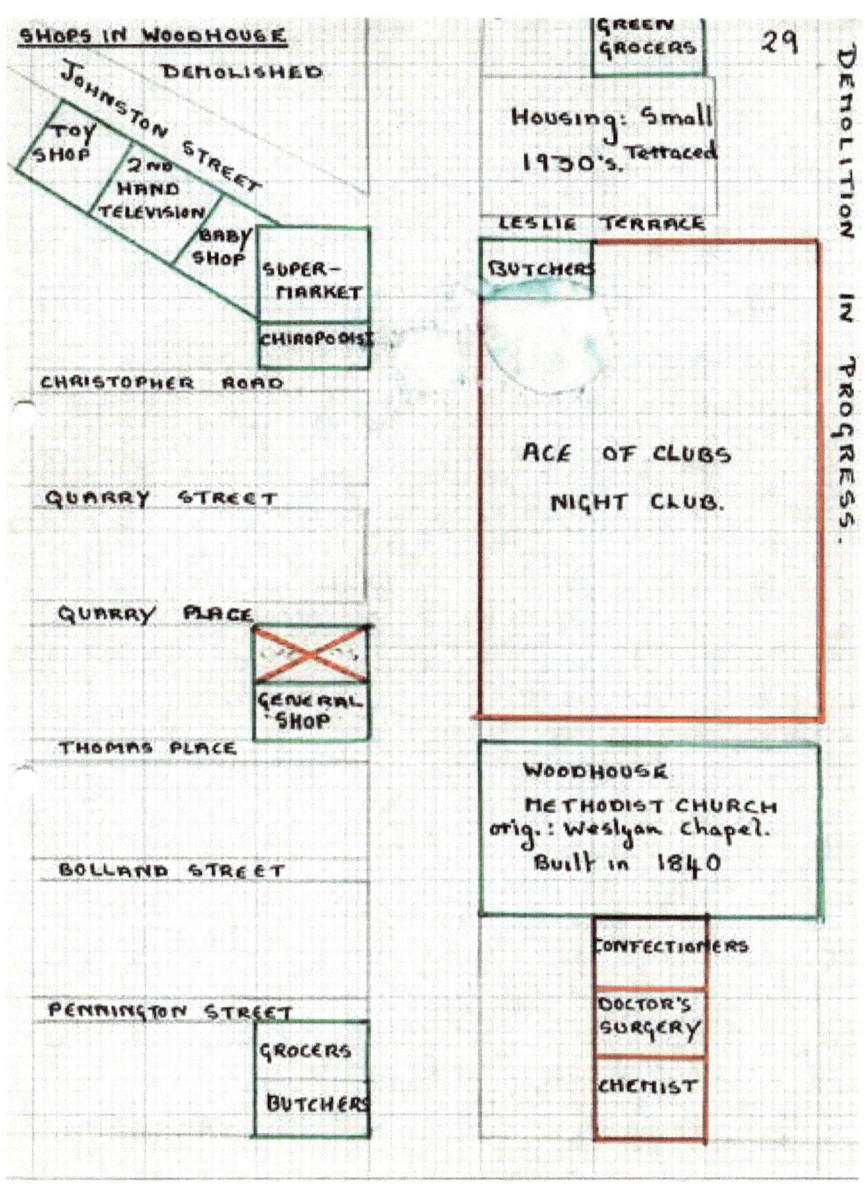

Map 29

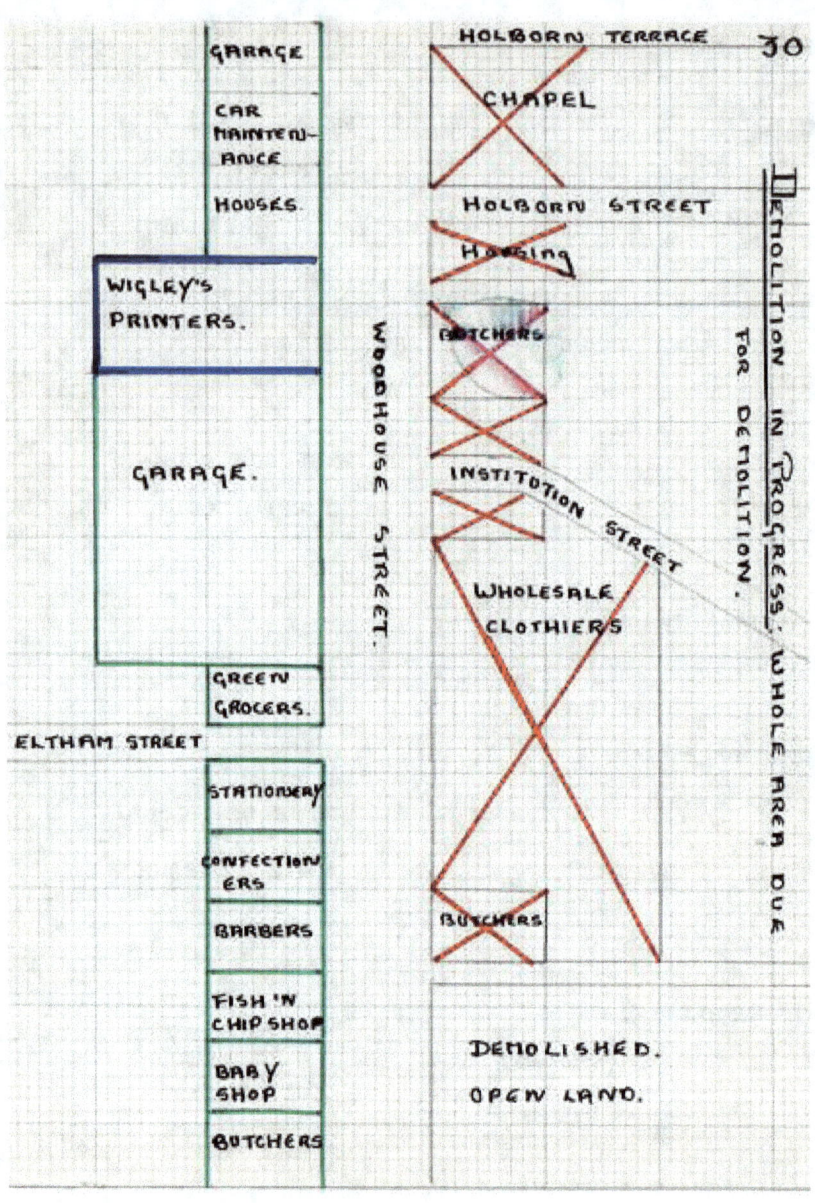

Map 30

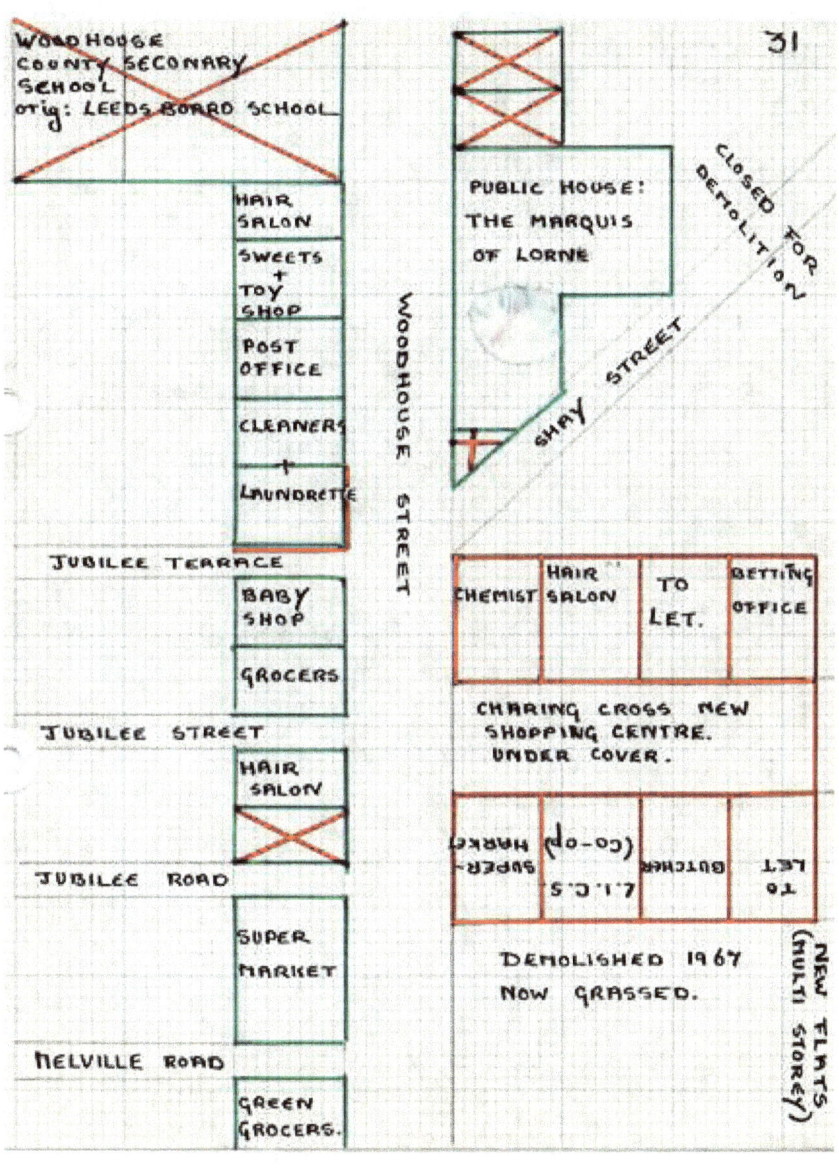

Map 31

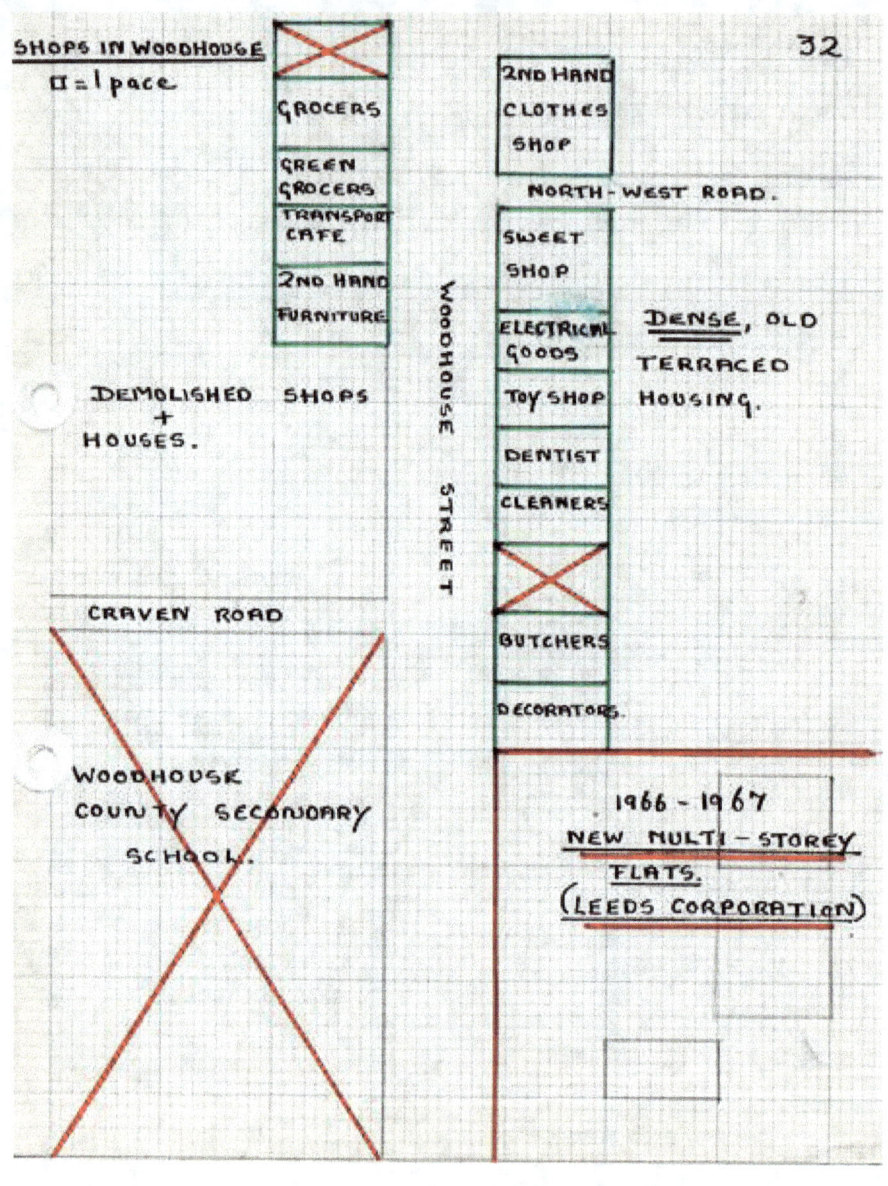

Map 32

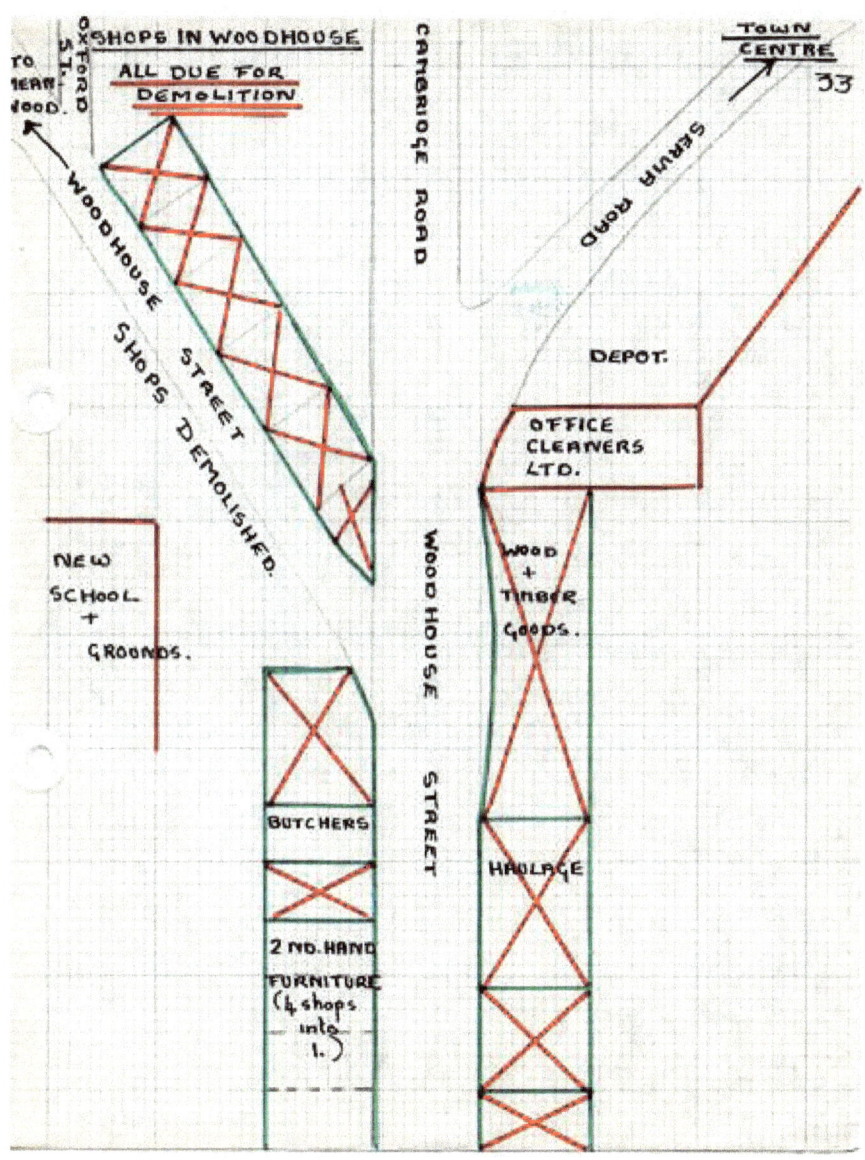

Map 33

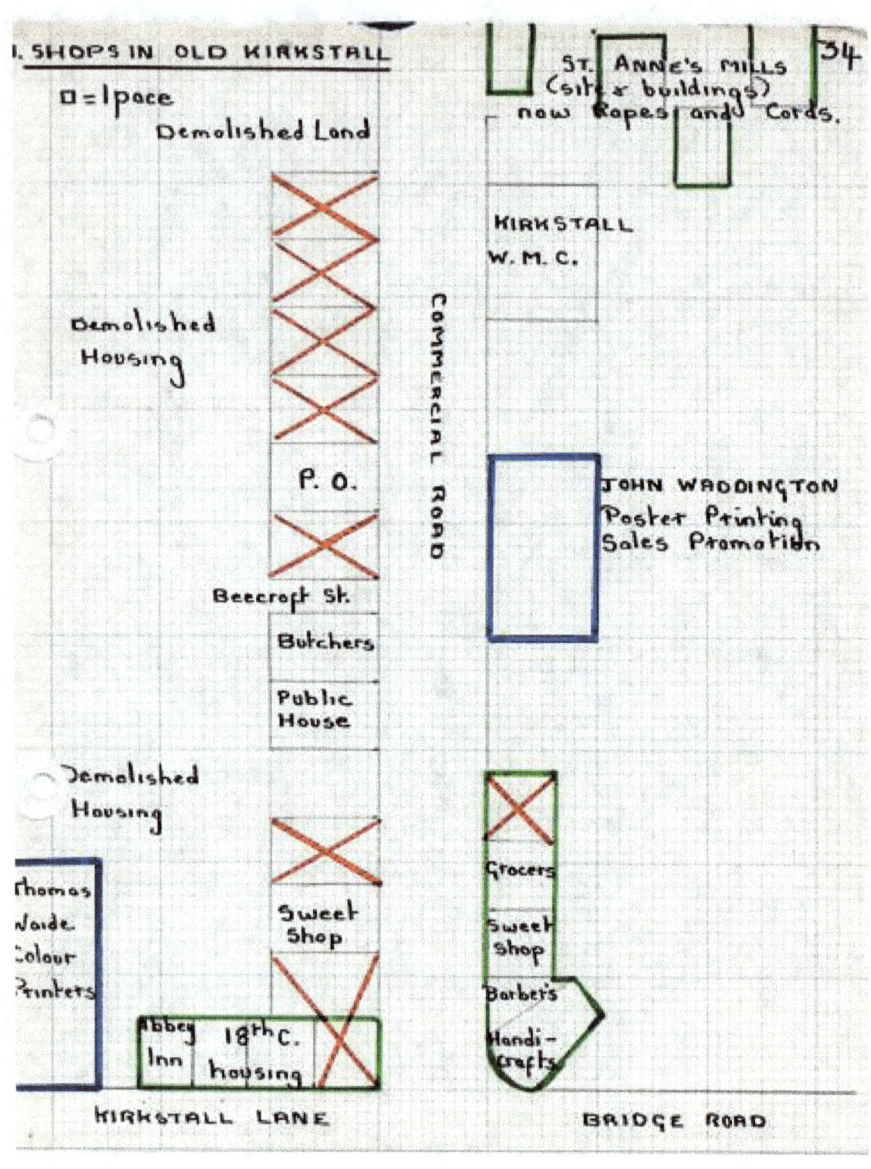

Map 34

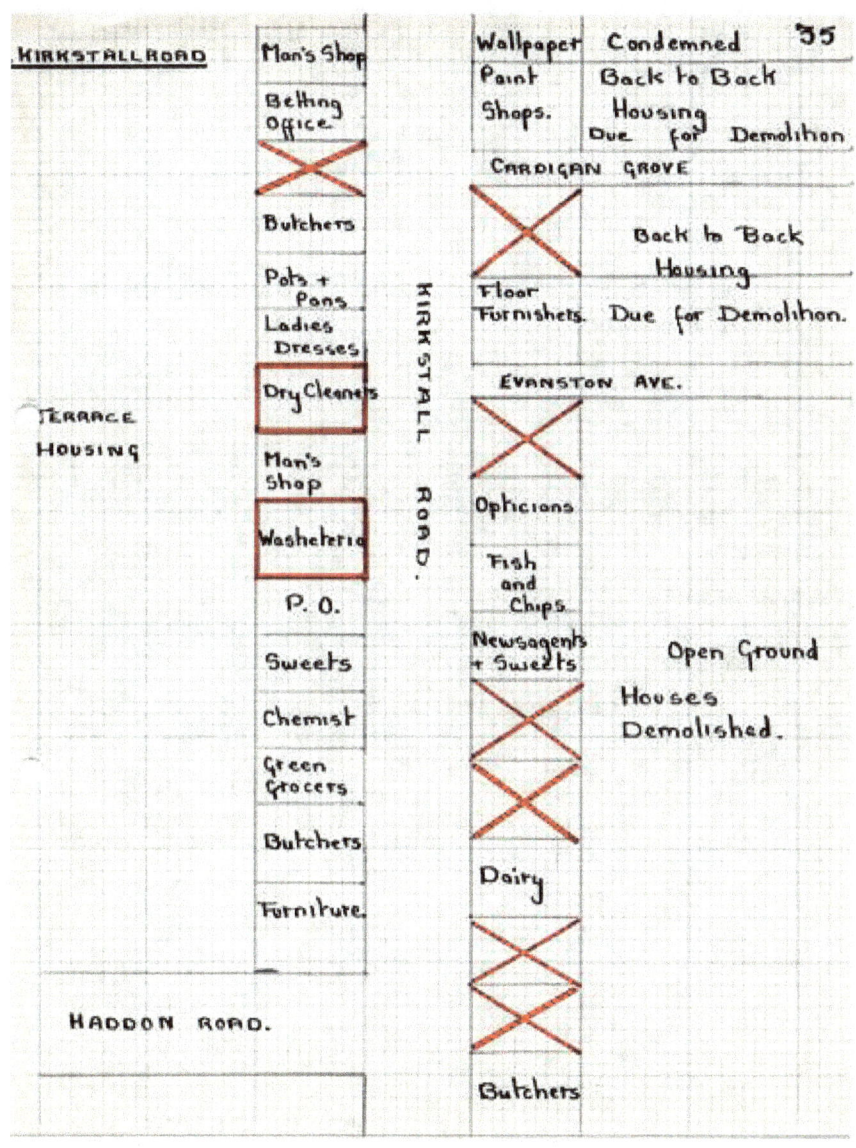

Map 35

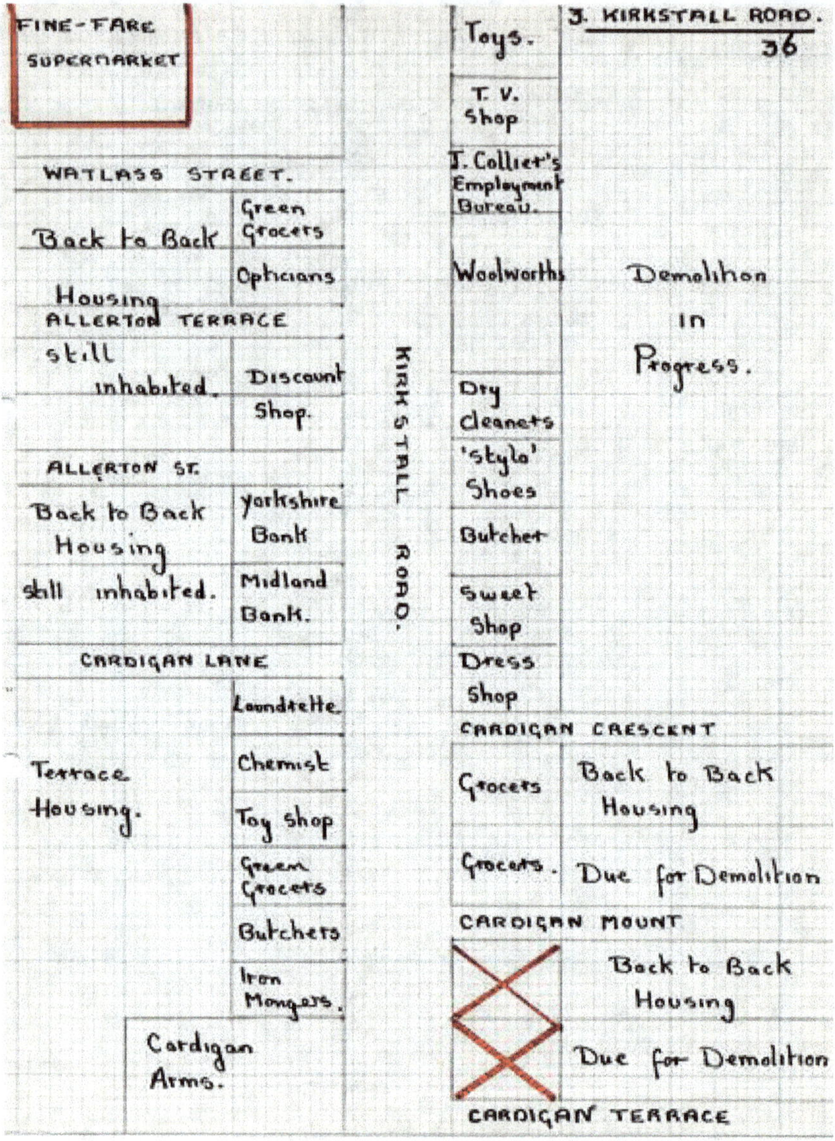

FINE-FARE SUPERMARKET			Toys.	J. KIRKSTALL ROAD. 36
			T.V. Shop	
WATLASS STREET.			J. Collier's Employment Bureau.	
Back to Back Housing	Green Grocers			
	Opticians		Woolworths	Demolition in Progress.
ALLERTON TERRACE still inhabited.	Discount Shop.	KIRKSTALL ROAD.	Dry Cleaners	
ALLERTON ST.			'Stylo' Shoes	
Back to Back Housing still inhabited.	Yorkshire Bank		Butcher	
	Midland Bank.		Sweet Shop	
CARDIGAN LANE			Dress Shop	
Terrace Housing.	Laundrette.		CARDIGAN CRESCENT	
	Chemist		Grocers	Back to Back Housing
	Toy shop		Grocers.	Due for Demolition
	Green Grocers		CARDIGAN MOUNT	
	Butchers		✗✗	Back to Back Housing
	Iron Mongers.		✗✗	Due for Demolition
Cardigan Arms.			CARDIGAN TERRACE	

Map 36

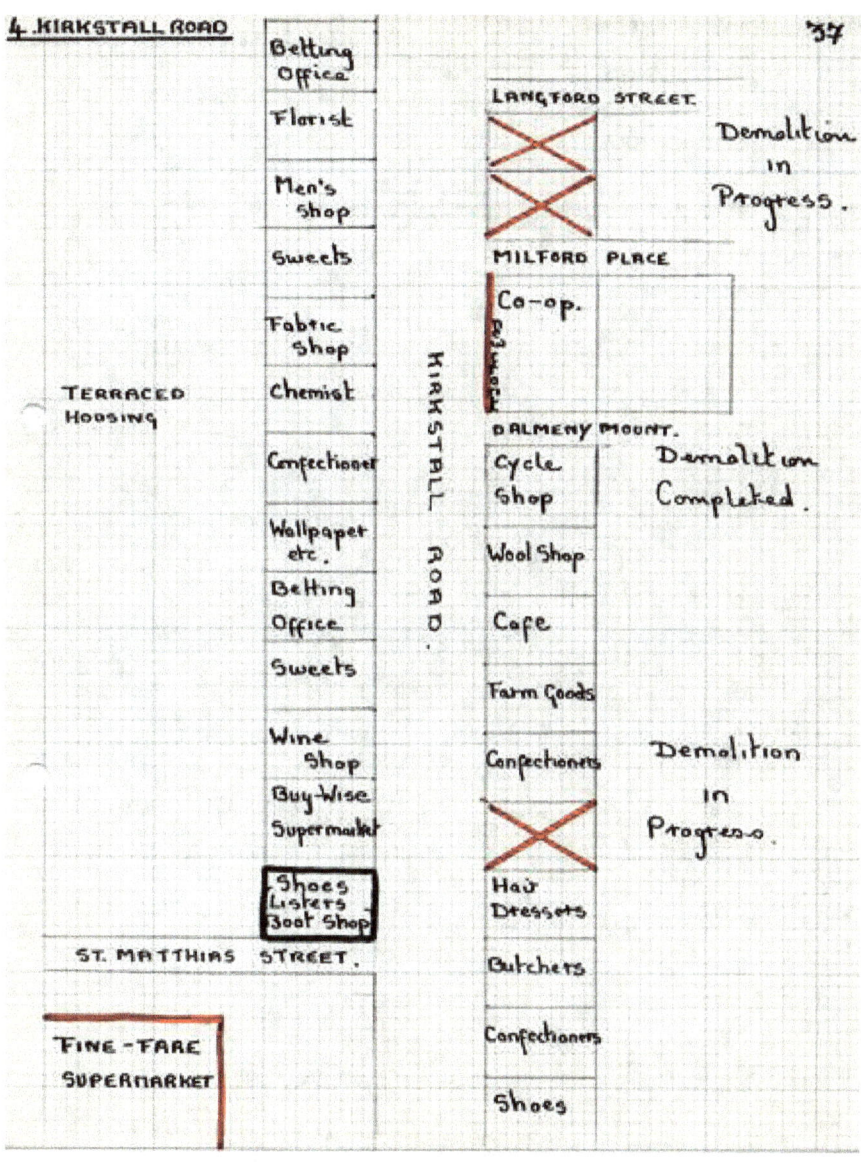

Map 37

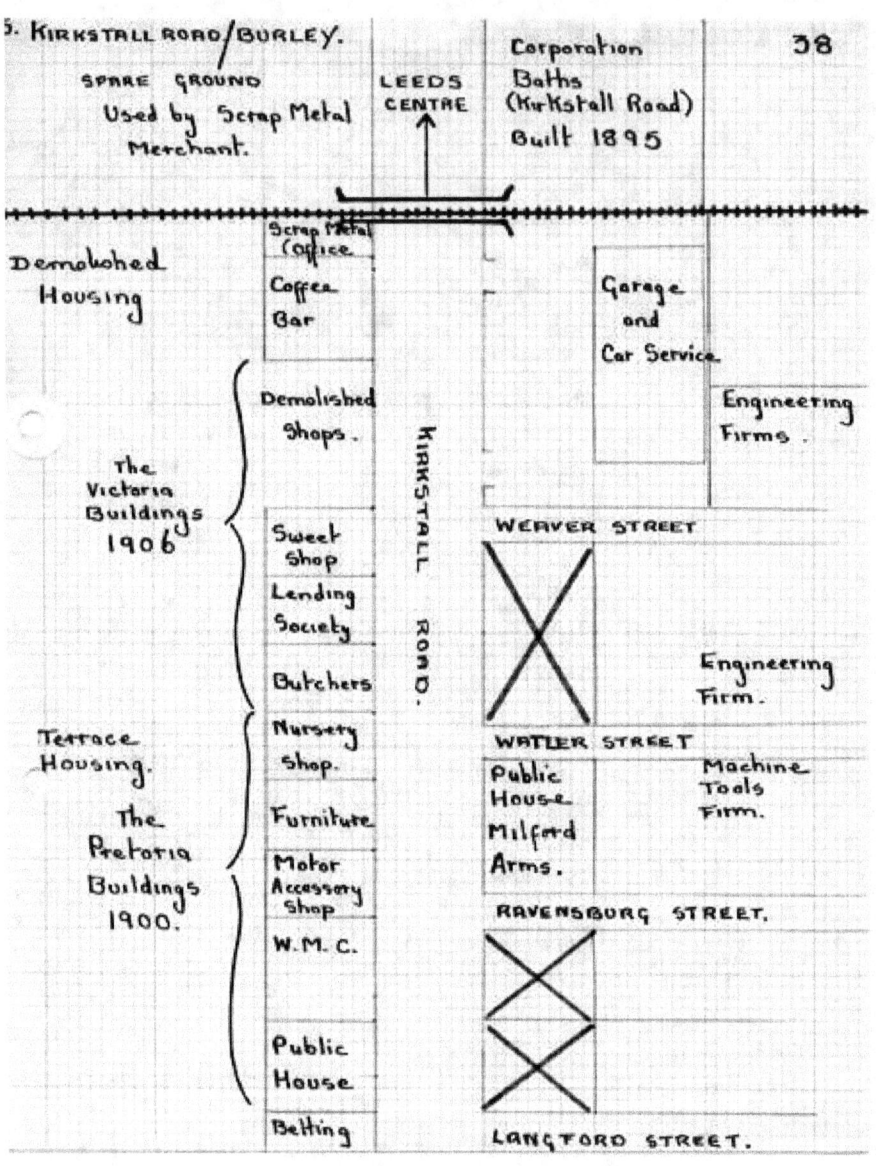

This pattern is adhered to in all the suburbs under study. Each suburb has its own shopping area along the main road, immediately on the road side. In Map 38 of Kirkstall, we see two terraces along the main Kirkstall Road. The shops are identical, all the same size and structure. One terrace of shops was built in 1900, the Pretoria Buildings; the other slightly later in 1906, the Victoria buildings. However, part of these have now been demolished.

The main shopping areas consisted mainly of small, independent food shops set up in order to make the suburb self-sufficient. There were no other types of shops – no shoe shops, clothes shops, or handicraft shops or such like. However, Headingley shopping centre was slightly different to the rule. High class, small shops were set up around 1850 and were mostly set up privately. They were not only grocery shops. Shops were of a kind where goods were made by craftsmen in the shops themselves and they sold their goods directly to their customers.

Shopkeepers in Headingley also sold imported goods. One shop - see Headingley Shops in Map 43 - is Groococks which began in 1860s and is still a prosperous business today. Groococks sold foreign fruits and spices. They still sell them today as well as branching out into confectionery. As Headingley developed, its shopping area grew, and it became a quite large, self-sufficient unit. It had banks, a Post Office, a library, a BOOTS chemist's, doctor's surgeries, tailor shops, book shops as well as the usual food shops catering for every need – butchers, bakers, grocers and so on. Headingley was also quite a refined area at the time where tea was taken at four in the afternoon and so a large number of bakeries and pastry shops emerged selling buns, cakes, and other delicacies. This trend still exists today. In the whole of Headingley there are sixteen confectioners 'cake shops, which is quite a large proportion devoted to one foodstuff. There are also several fish and chip shops. Entertainment is provided by the Lounge cinema in North Lane, as well as the numerous public houses such as The Original Oak and the Skyrack.

In the lower class suburbs, the shops were more like open stalls. A greengrocer's in Burley - see Map 42, on the corner of Burley Road and Hyde Park Road still displays its goods out on the street, like a stall. This shop was established in 1908.

The working classes were first introduced to retail trade by the Co-operative Movement. The main branch of the Co-operative opened in 1884 and there was a sudden boom in this kind of shop so that by 1900, seventy other branches had opened up. There is a Co-op (as they were later called) in Headingley (L. I. C. S.) - see Map 45 which has recently been given a new more modern frontage. Another Co-op is in Kirkstall, see Map 37. This Co-op is on the corner of a street and is two shops converted into one. The surrounding area is now in the process of being demolished, so the future of this Co-op branch looks rather bleak. From general observations of the Maps of the Shopping Facilities, they clearly fall into two main categories: 1. the old shops (in green) and 2. those shops boarded up (with a red diagonal cross). This situation is expected as the residential areas are old and uninhabited, the shops were built at the same time as the houses to serve the residents.

The worst old shops are in Kirkstall, Burley and Woodhouse. There is over repetition of the same types of shops; for example, in one part of Kirkstall within a hundred yards of each other on both sides of the road, there are four grocer's shops, whilst a few shops further on, there is a Fine Fair Supermarket, a Buy wise Supermarket and the Co-op all selling groceries. The planning and distribution of the types of shops has become completely unbalanced. This is partially due to the selling-new ownership and re-selling of these shops that has continued over the years. Besides, the new, larger supermarkets were becoming increasingly popular. Some of the older shops that would have naturally closed down, stayed open by becoming places to sell second-hand furniture and second-hand books – see Map 28 and second hand clothes see Map 32. In order to sell furniture and larger bulky goods, the small old shops have been knocked through so that four or five shops now form one long shop - see Map 33 of Woodhouse. However, the older shops that are still in good condition and in a residential area where there is a lot of custom, have been modernised bringing the shops up to the required standard.

In the past so many parades of shops developed that today, quite a large proportion of them have had to close up; competition from more modern, neighbouring shops and the improved City central shopping area have proved too great. Also, of course there has been so much slum clearance and a shift of population that there is only a small amount of custom left for a very large number of shops, so naturally many owners have closed business and moved to the new shopping areas. Most of these shops are too old and not up to standard to be re-sold, so they have been boarded up, awaiting demolition.

Woodhouse has suffered the greatest loss of population and respectively the greatest number of shops to be boarded up. From Map 53 we can see that Woodhouse has 31 shops boarded up at the present time. A small new shopping centre has been built in Woodhouse, see Map 31, known as Charing Cross Shopping Centre. This centre was built at the same time as the nearby blocks of multi-storey flats, in order to serve that area. It is a limited shopping area and as can be seen from the map, two of the eight shops are still to let. This is the only shopping development in Woodhouse, but it was not really needed because it already had more than enough shops and it is also within easy reach of the city centre.

From Map 53, Kirkstall has 25 shops boarded up and waiting for demolition and most of the shops still open and in use will have been demolished by 1981. From Map 34 we see the shops in the village site of Kirkstall at the bottom of the map. These shops, five of which are still open, are tiny stone built village shops with large stone slab roofs, a small door, and small windows. These are all due for demolition.

Burley has 20 shops boarded up and the reason the number is so high is because a whole parade of 10 shops is boarded up - see Map 39. These have been boarded up for at least ten years.

The most significant point about Map 53 is the fact that Headingley has no shops boarded up at all. Headingley has always been a large thriving shopping area, one in Headingley itself and the other in Far Headingley with a small terrace of six shops lying between these two areas.

Headingley now has a new role as the main shopping area for Burley, Kirkstall, Lawnswood, West Park, Adel and Bramhope. Its role is to serve this large area so more shops were needed. In the 1960s Headingley took on many changes mainly development in its shopping facilities so that it was able to serve this large district (1961-1981 plan).

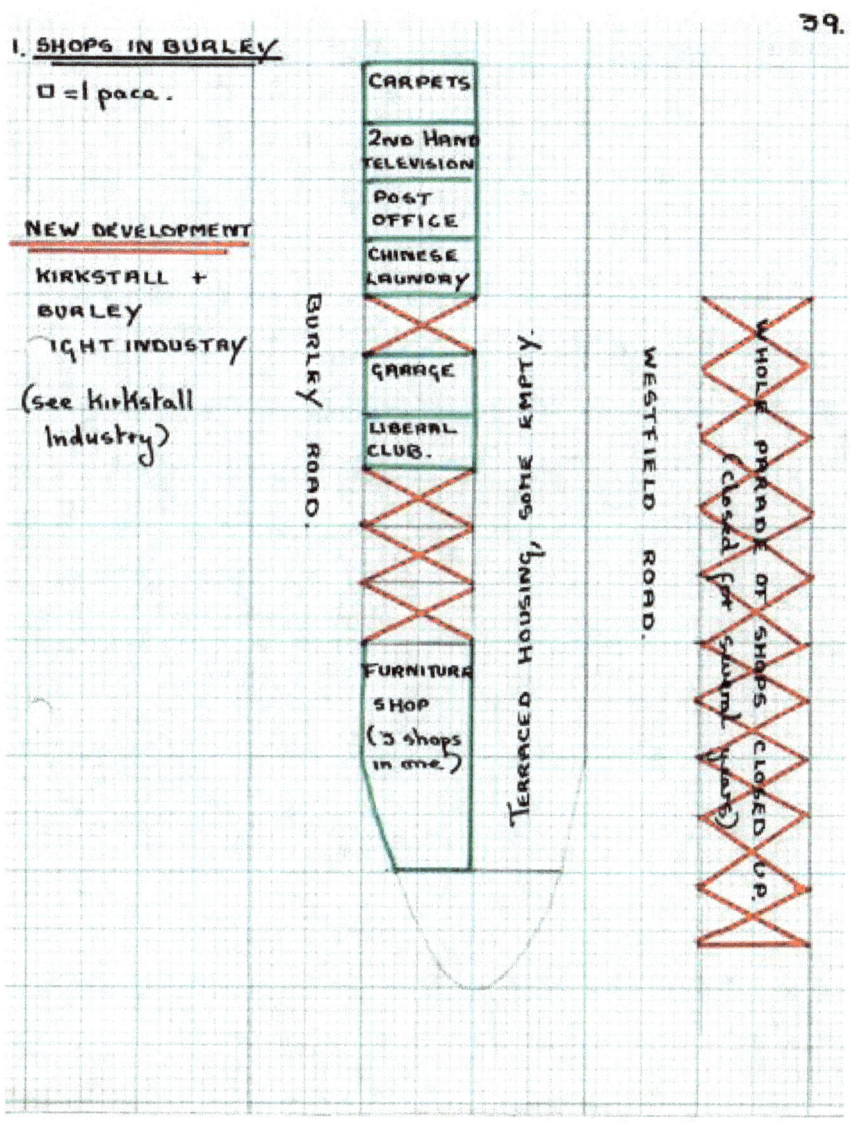

Map 39

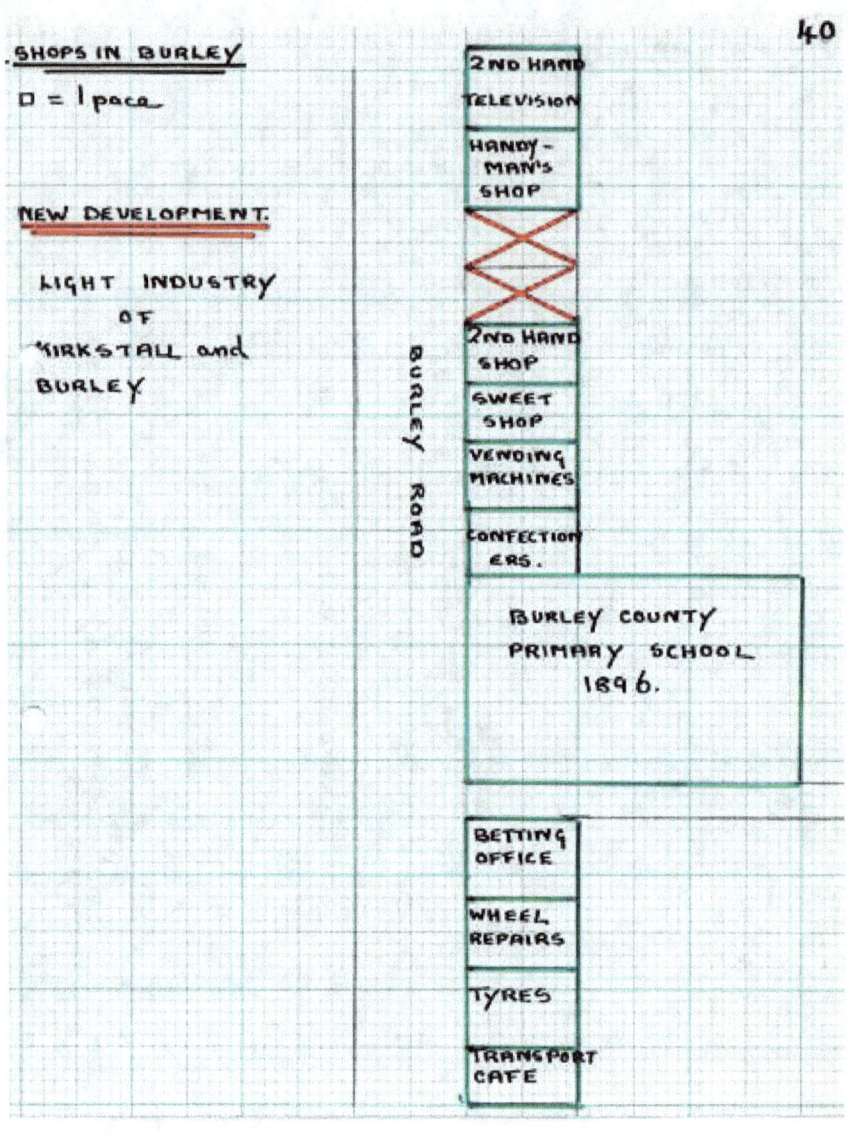

Map 40

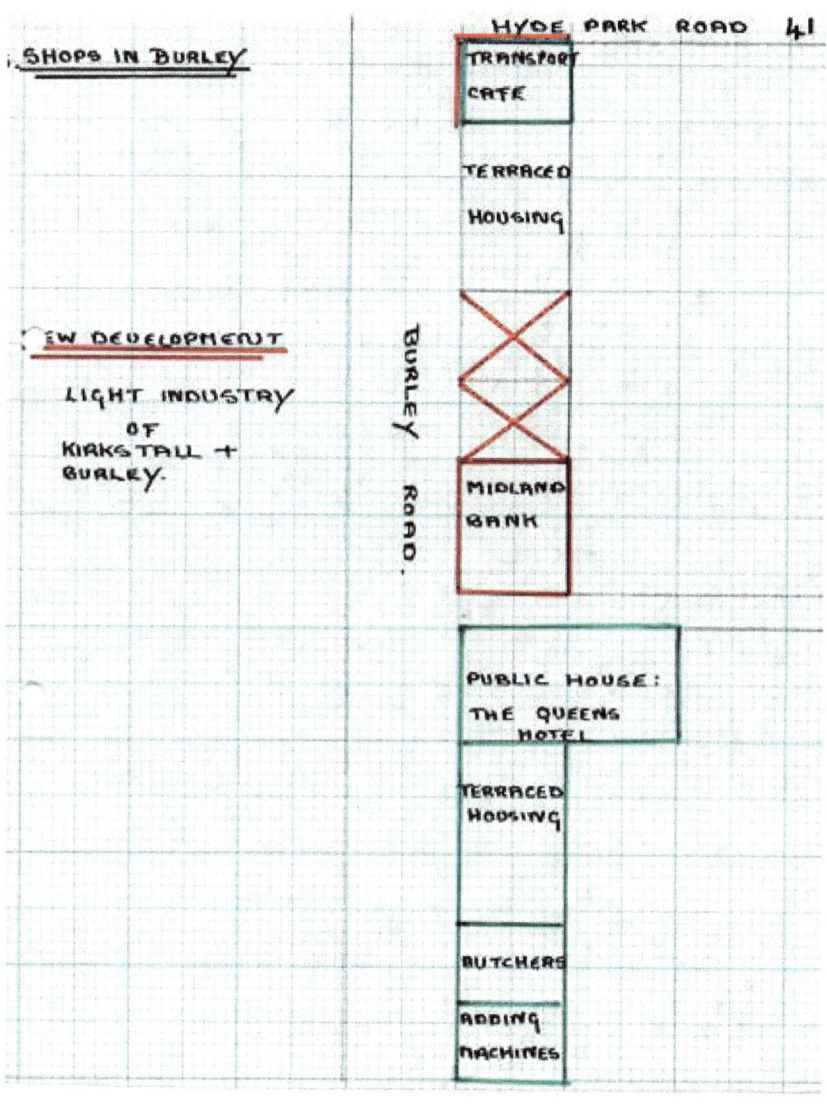

Map 41

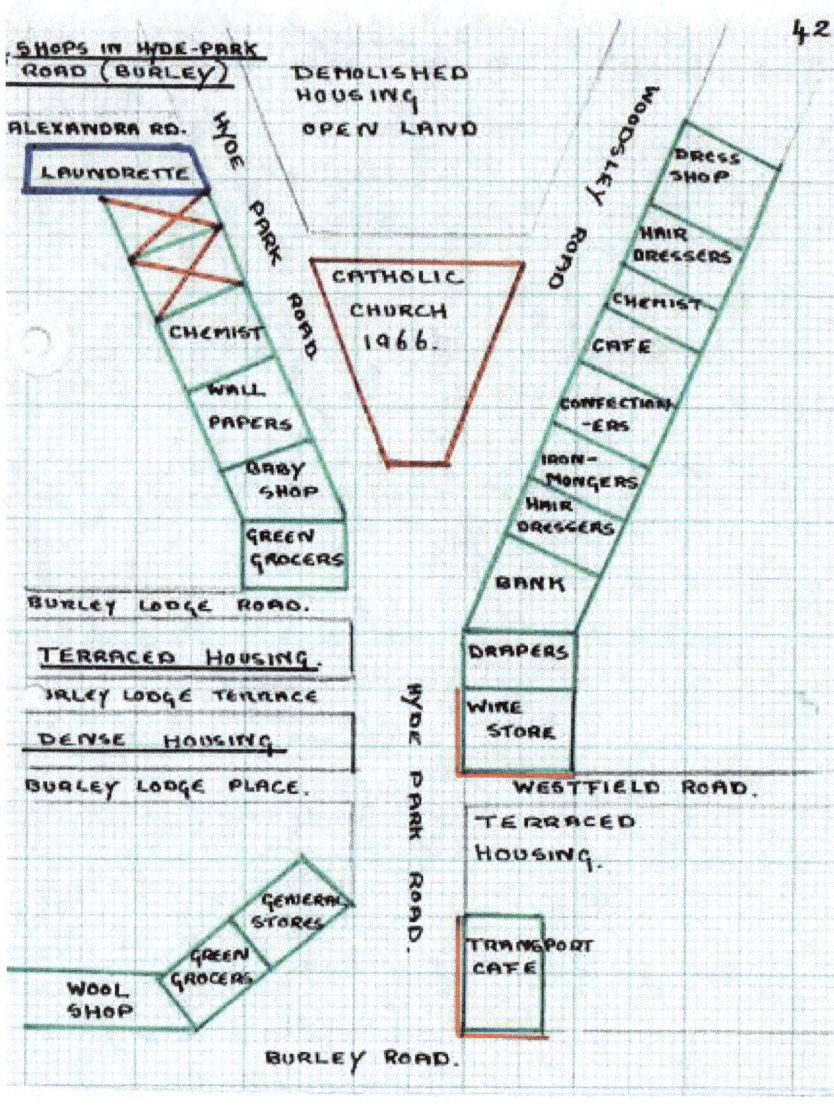

Map 42

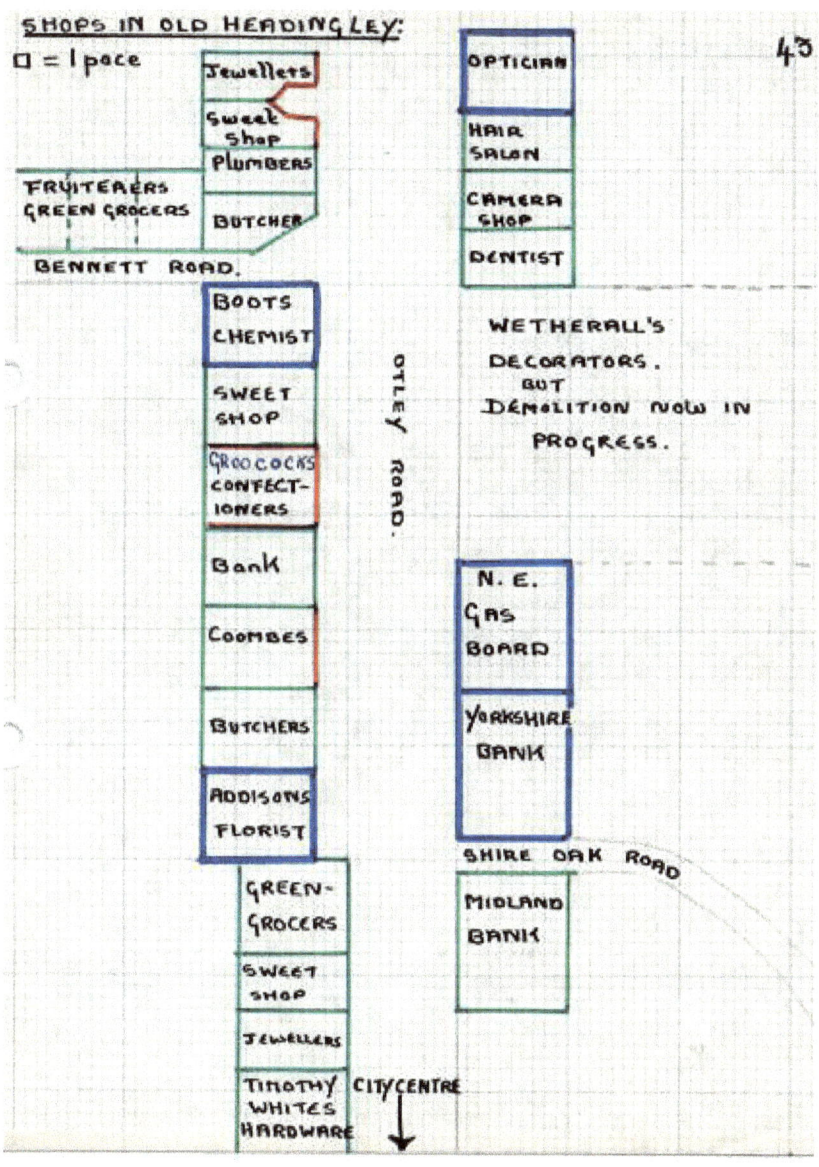

Map 43

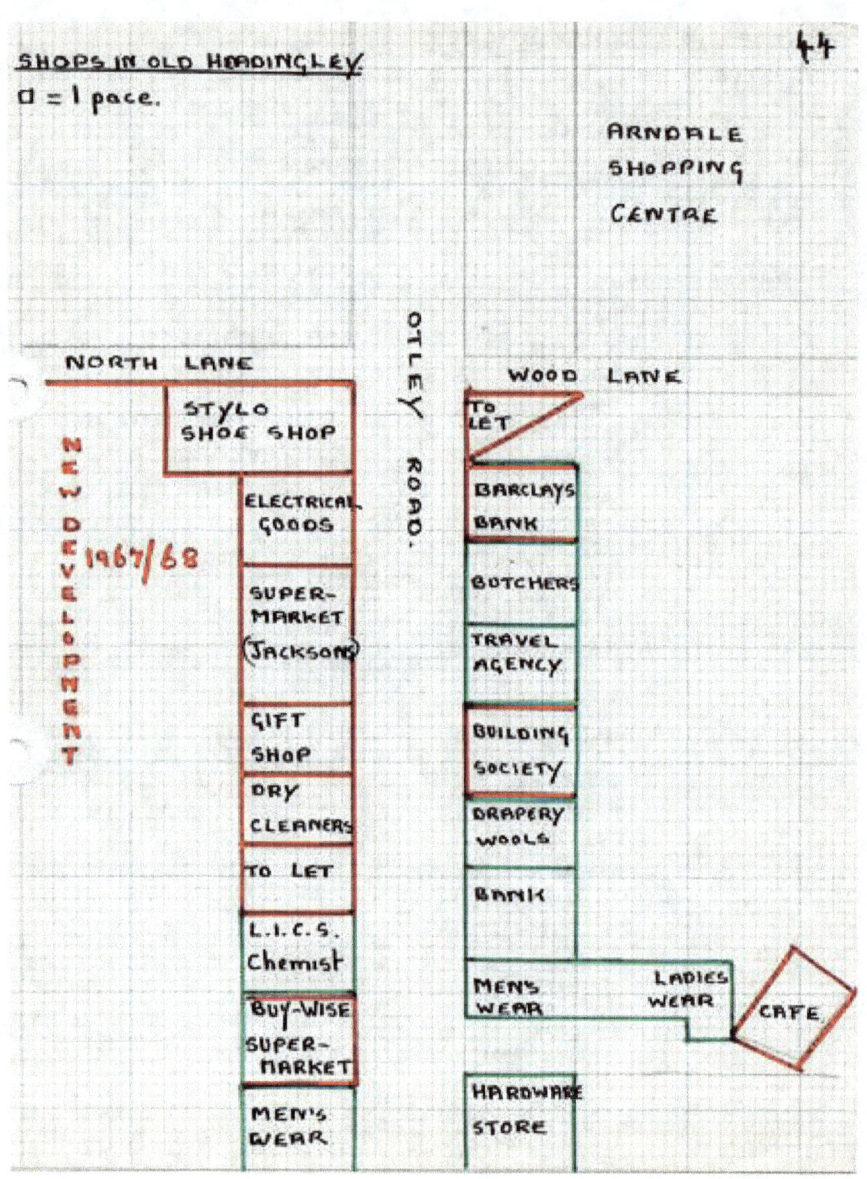

Map 44

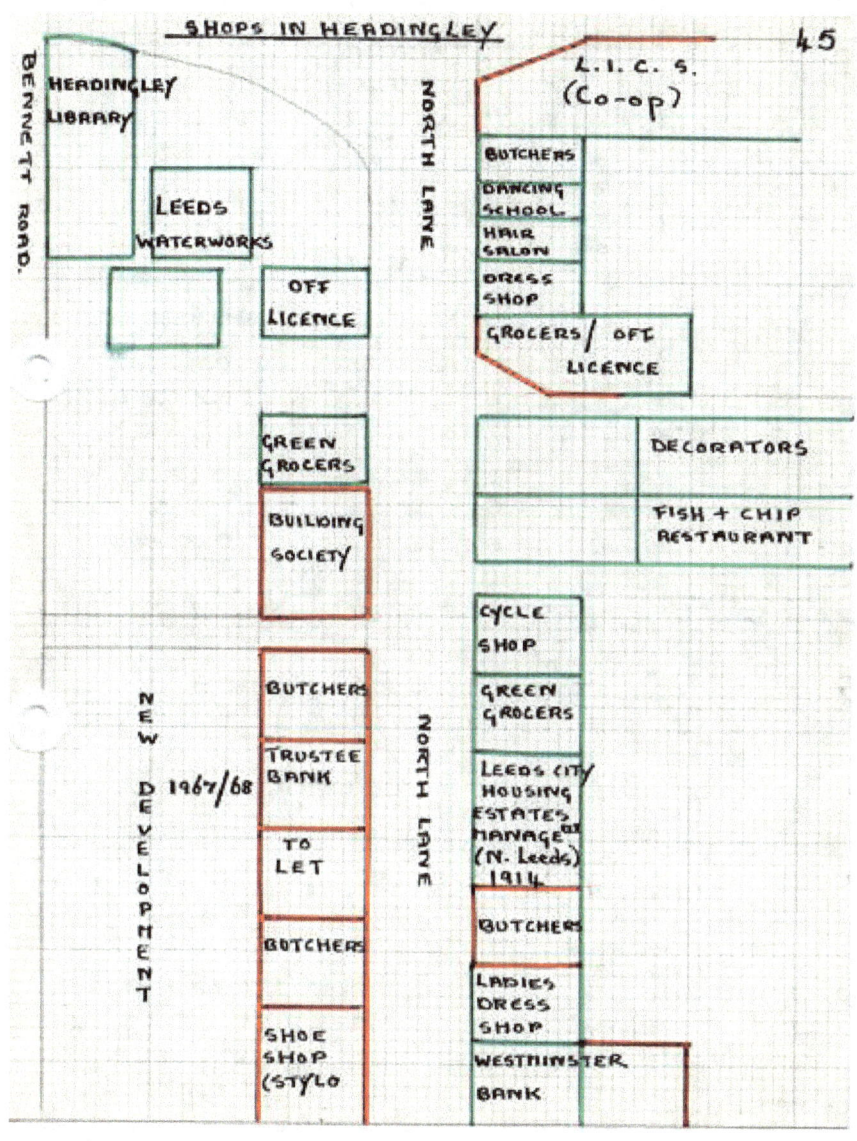

Map 45

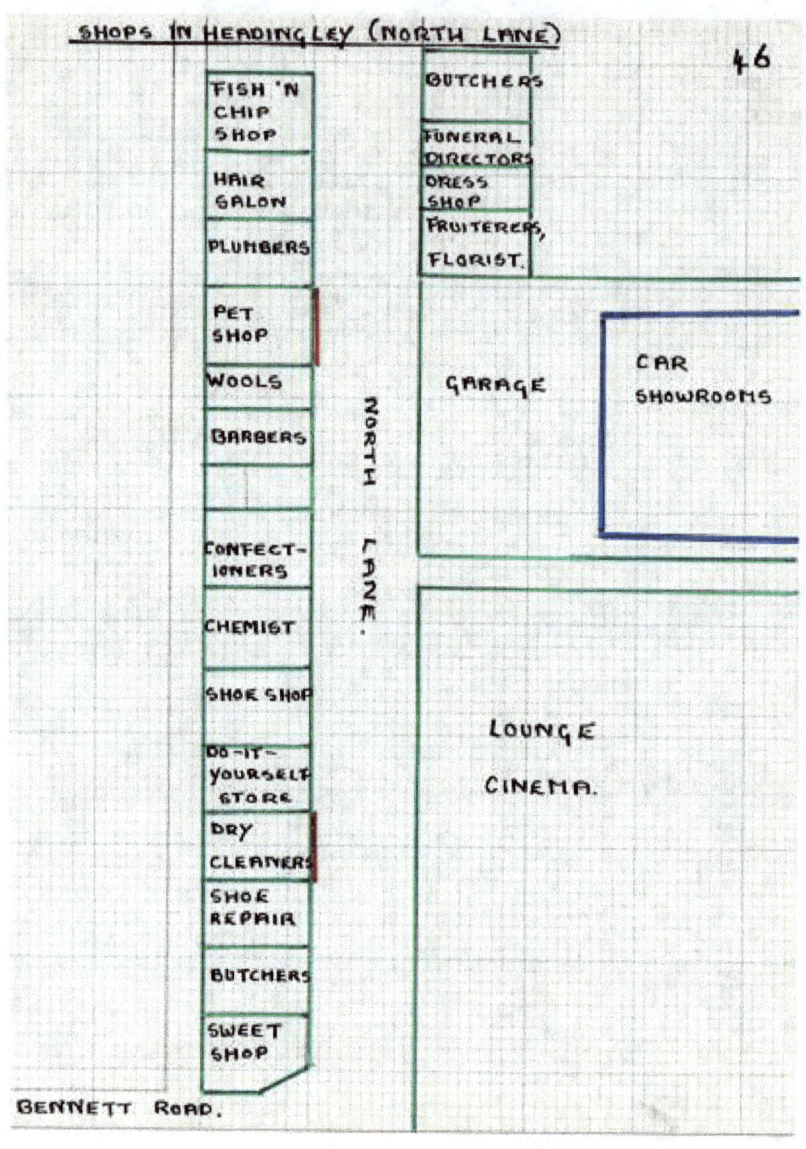

Map 46

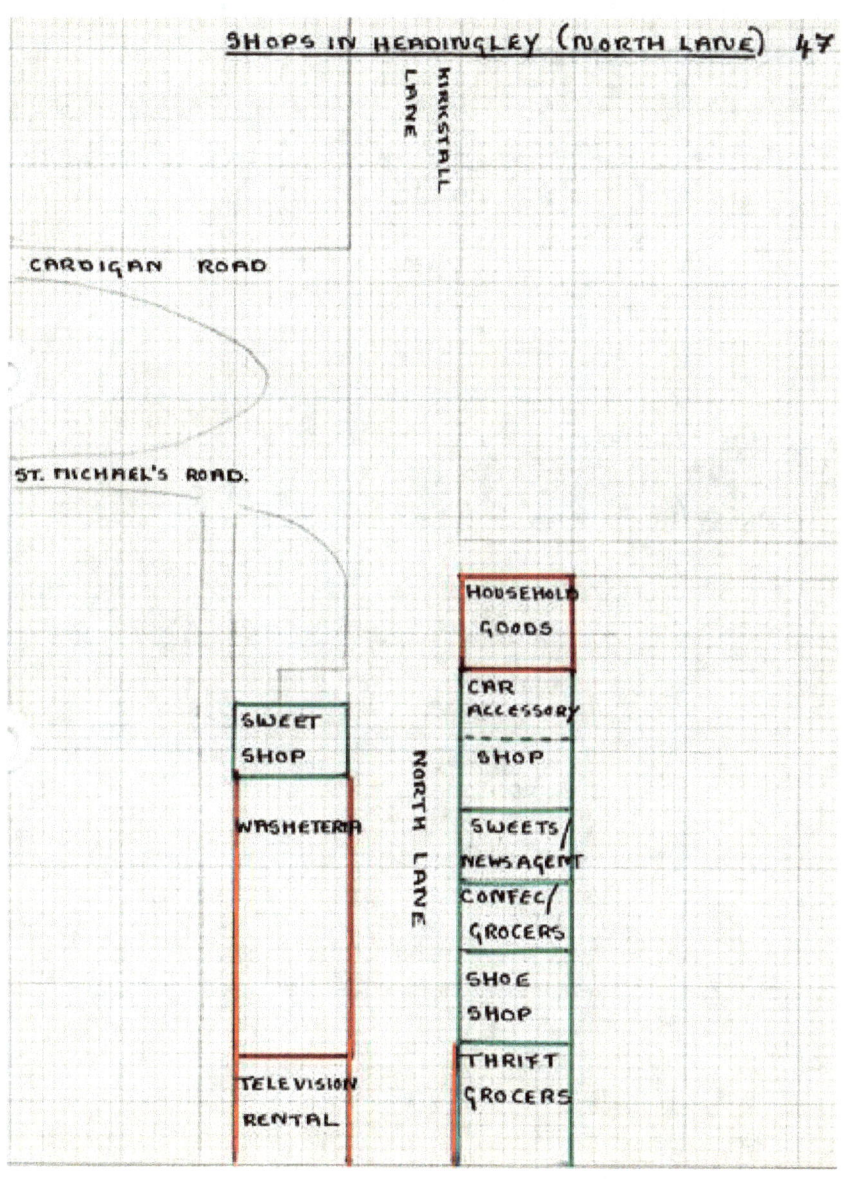

Map 47

Shops in Headingley:

New Development: The Arndale Shopping Centre

This was the FIRST ARNDALE CENTRE to be built in Leeds; completed in 1967.

SCALE: □ = 1 pace.

```
WOOD LANE
TOP RANK BOWLING
ALLEY (NOW CLOSED)
                    Entrance
        ┌─────────────┬──────────────┐
        │  FRIED      │              │
        │  CHICKEN    │              │
        │     SHOP    │              │
        ├─────────────┤  SHOPPING    │
        │  ELECTRICAL │  UNDER       │   OTLEY ROAD.
        │  GOODS      │  COVER.      │
        ├─────────────┤              │
        │ DISCOUNT STORE│            │
        ├─────────────┤              │
        │ CONFECTIONERS│             │
        ├─────────────┤              │
        │  TO  LET    │              │
        ├─────────────┤              │
        │ DRY CLEANERS│              │
        └─────────────┴──────────────┘
```

Map 48

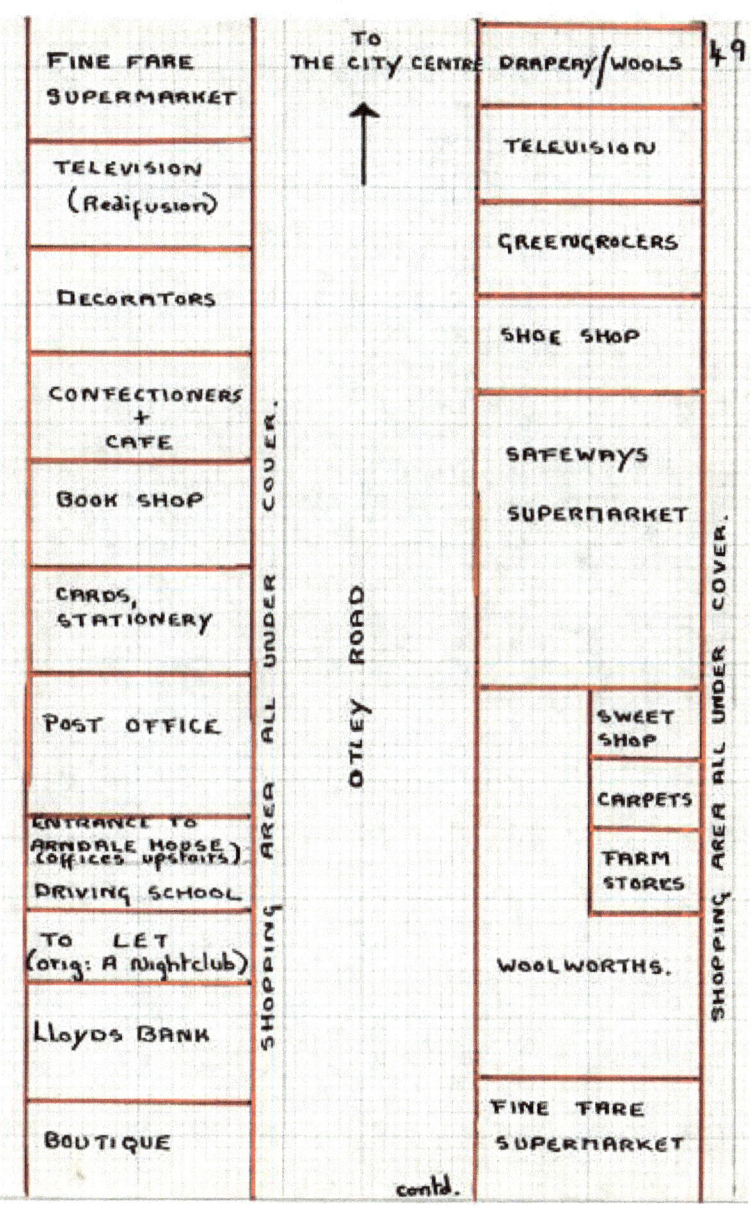

Map 49

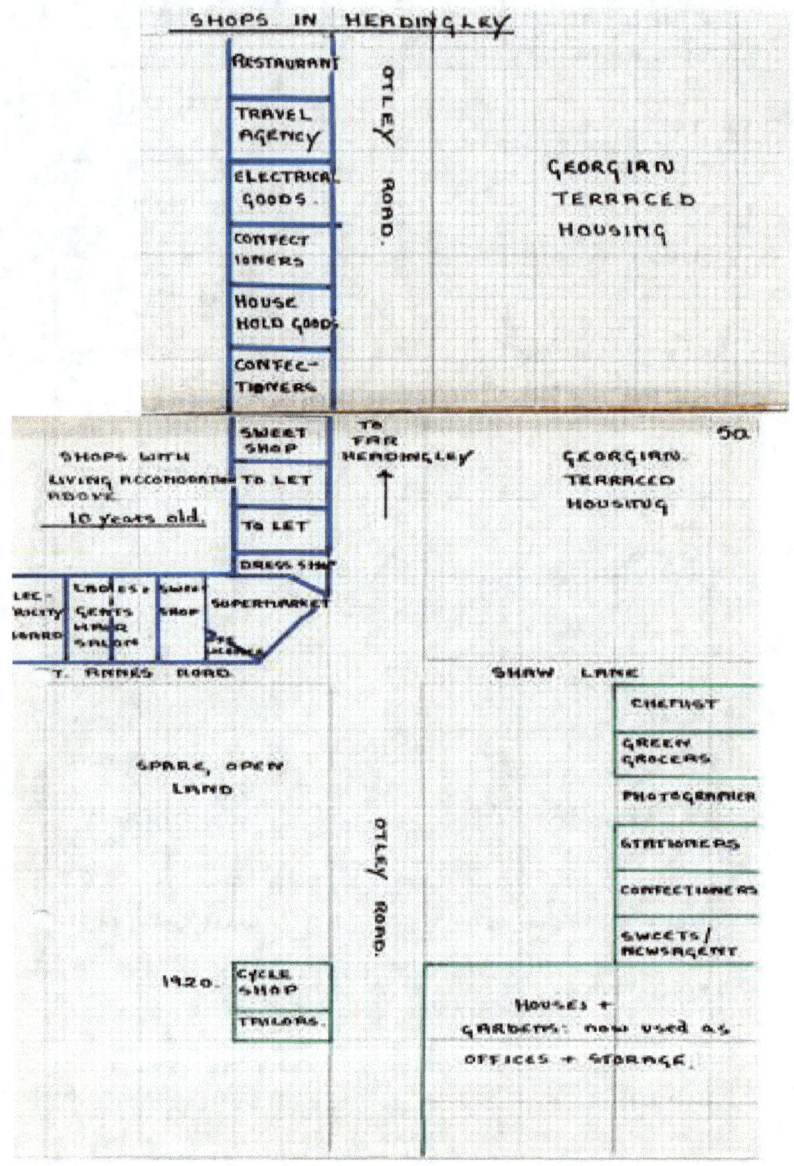

Map 50

The first development was the Arndale shopping Centre. Maps 48 and 49. This was the first Arndale Centre to be built in Leeds (others were being built in other big cities); it opened in1967. There are now similar centres in many other parts of Leeds, for example there is a large centre in Seacroft.

The Arndale Centre in Headingley is a long stretch of shops providing a balanced variety of stuffs, also a bank and a large Post Office. One of the most noticeable points are the three supermarkets which emphasises the current shopping trend. The Supermarkets - Fine Fare, Safeways and Woolworths – are all next to one another and they form the biggest shops in the centre.

The other shops are mediocre in size, they have a modern style with large glass windows. The pavement along the shopping area is covered A modern invention to make shopping more pleasant especially on rainy days. The Centre's second storey also caters for Headingley entertainment. A nightclub was built and was popular for a short time, but it did not receive enough trade and closed in 1968. At the other end of the centre (Map 48) there is the Top Rank Bowling Alley, but due to trouble and vandalism this was also closed in 1969.

In the lower half of Headingley's old shopping area, the shops were demolished to make way for a new shopping development (Map 44 and 45). This development was completed in 1968 after the Arndale Centre; completion was delayed it seems due to fire. Two of the shop units in the Headingley Centre are still to let. It has two supermarkets: Buywise and Jacksons. All the supermarkets seem to have a good deal of trade even if they are in abundance. Headingley District Shopping Centre has a branch of every bank and several Building societies making it a suburb of business and finance.

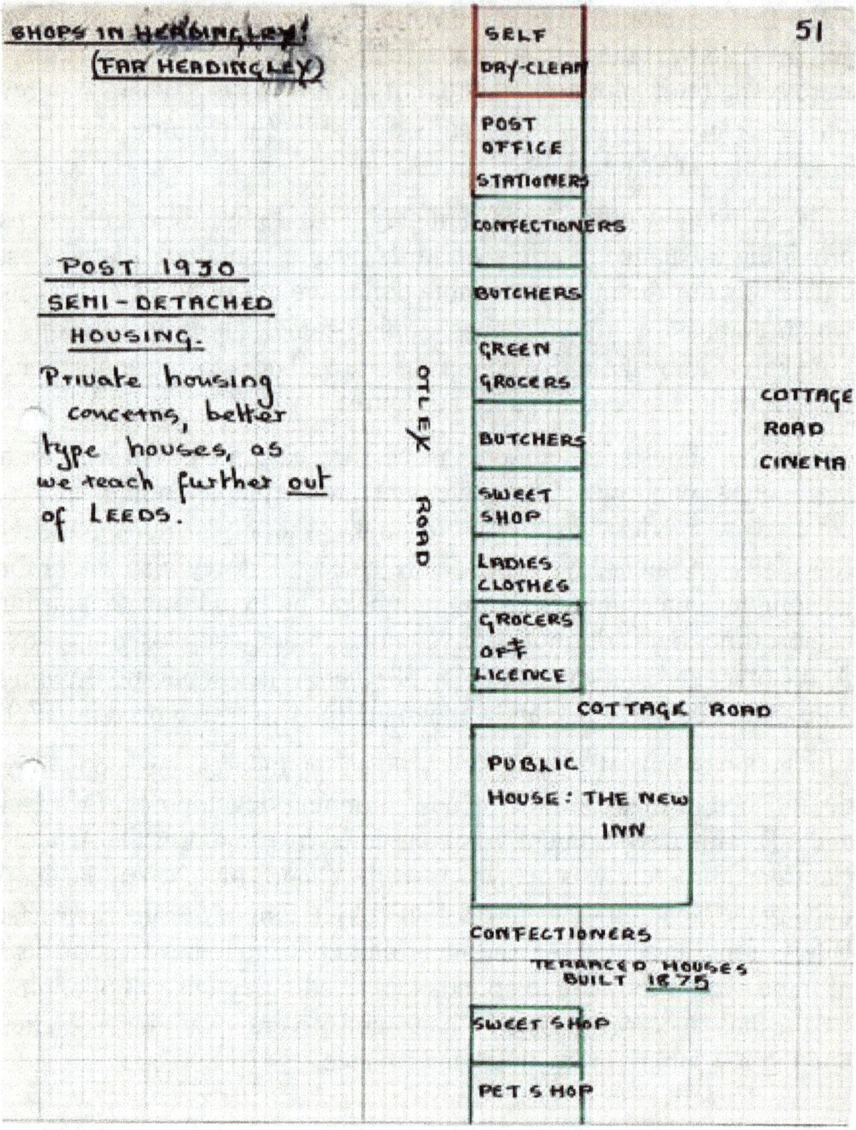

SHOPS IN HEADINGLEY
(FAR HEADINGLEY)   51

POST 1930
SEMI-DETACHED
HOUSING.

Private housing
concerns, better
type houses, as
we reach further out
of LEEDS.

SELF DRY-CLEAN	
POST OFFICE STATIONERS	
CONFECTIONERS	
BUTCHERS	
GREEN GROCERS	
BUTCHERS	
SWEET SHOP	
LADIES CLOTHES	
GROCERS OFF LICENCE	

OTLEY ROAD

COTTAGE ROAD CINEMA

COTTAGE ROAD

PUBLIC HOUSE: THE NEW INN

CONFECTIONERS
TERRACED HOUSES BUILT 1875
SWEET SHOP
PET SHOP

Map 51

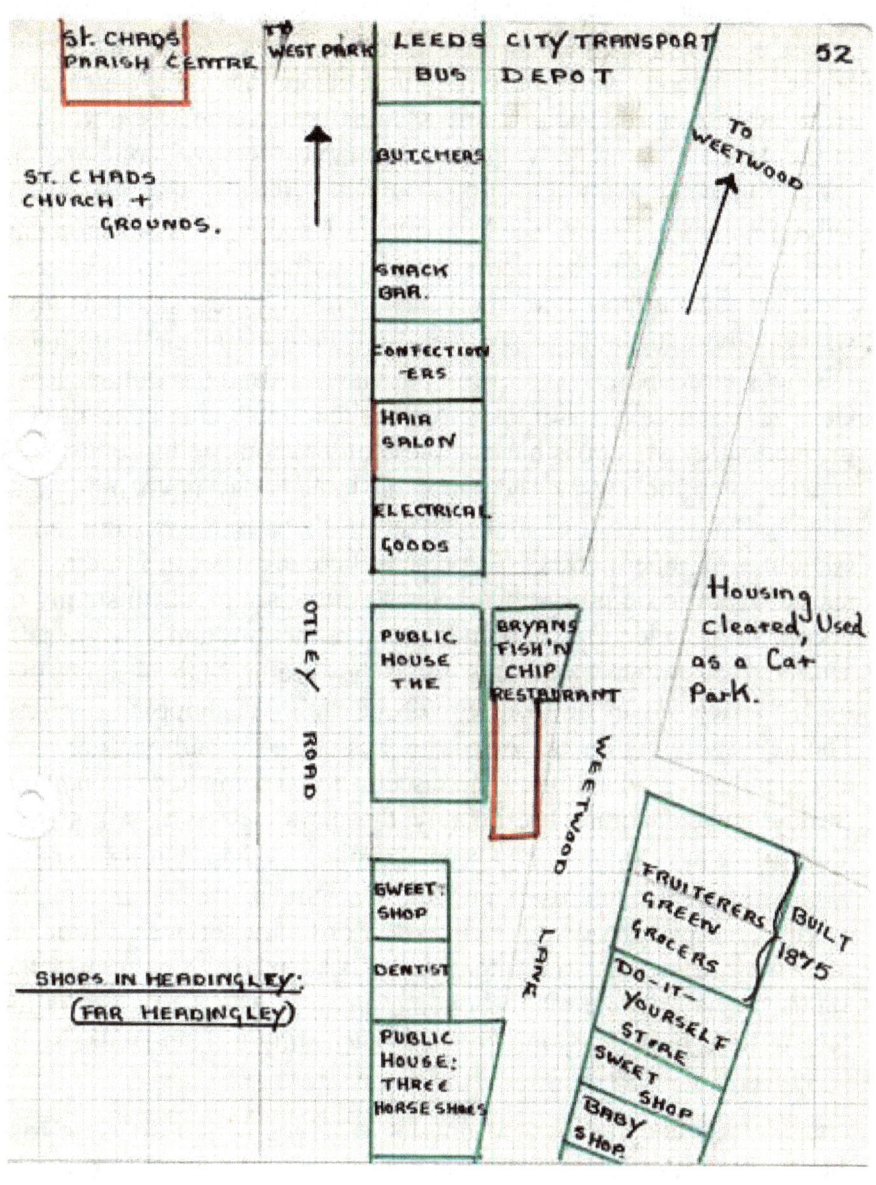

Map 52

In the mid shopping area between Headingley and Far Headingley, a series of shops were built about ten years ago, see Map 50. This group of shops serve those living in the Beckett Park area with household goods but more detailed shopping is done in the Headingley Centre. These shops are smaller in comparison to those in the Arndale Centre. Living accommodation is provided above the shops. On the opposite side of the road is the old shopping area which will remain as it is now - see Map 50. Far Headingley's old shopping area is not going to be modernised, it will continue to exist as a provider of household and emergency goods - a local shopping area, whereas the main bulk of shopping will be done in the Headingley District Centre. It also has several popular pubs and the Cottage Road Cinema. Eventually, with the shopping facilities being concentrated in Headingley, it is possible that these older shops will lose business and be forced to close. The shopping trend today is changing and moving away from the small private businesses toward the larger combines of supermarkets. At present there are a lot in Headingley, and all seem to be prosperous because there is a plentiful supply of goods, ample selections of brands, good reductions and they are self-service so customers choose the goods they prefer. Map 54 shows that by 1981 Headingley and Burley will be the main shopping districts. The new shopping centre for Burley has not been built yet nor have any plan been made public. There seems to be some hesitation about Burley's type of future. Presumably, the shopping centre will be built after the re development has been completed. There will be express transport routes to and from the main shopping districts, based on the original turnpike roads, as well as the ordinary services. From the Map we can see that the intention is to keep to the pattern of the 1800s, by having one main shopping area but it will be a centre for several suburbs; there won't be one in each suburb. There will also be several small, localised shops, the corner shops.

It is in this chapter that Headingley emerges with a different role thus making it different to the other suburbs. Headingley has lost its air of a purely residential, high class suburb and has become a modern busy centre serving a large area extending out of the Leeds boundary.

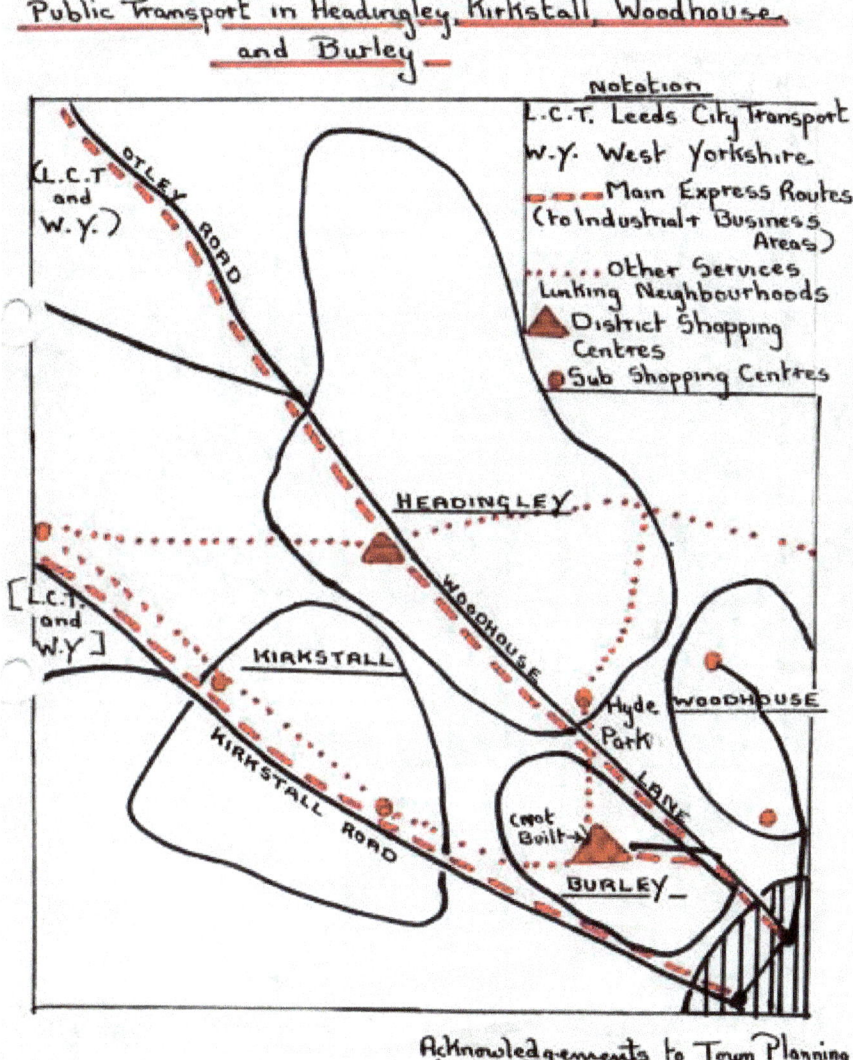

Map 53

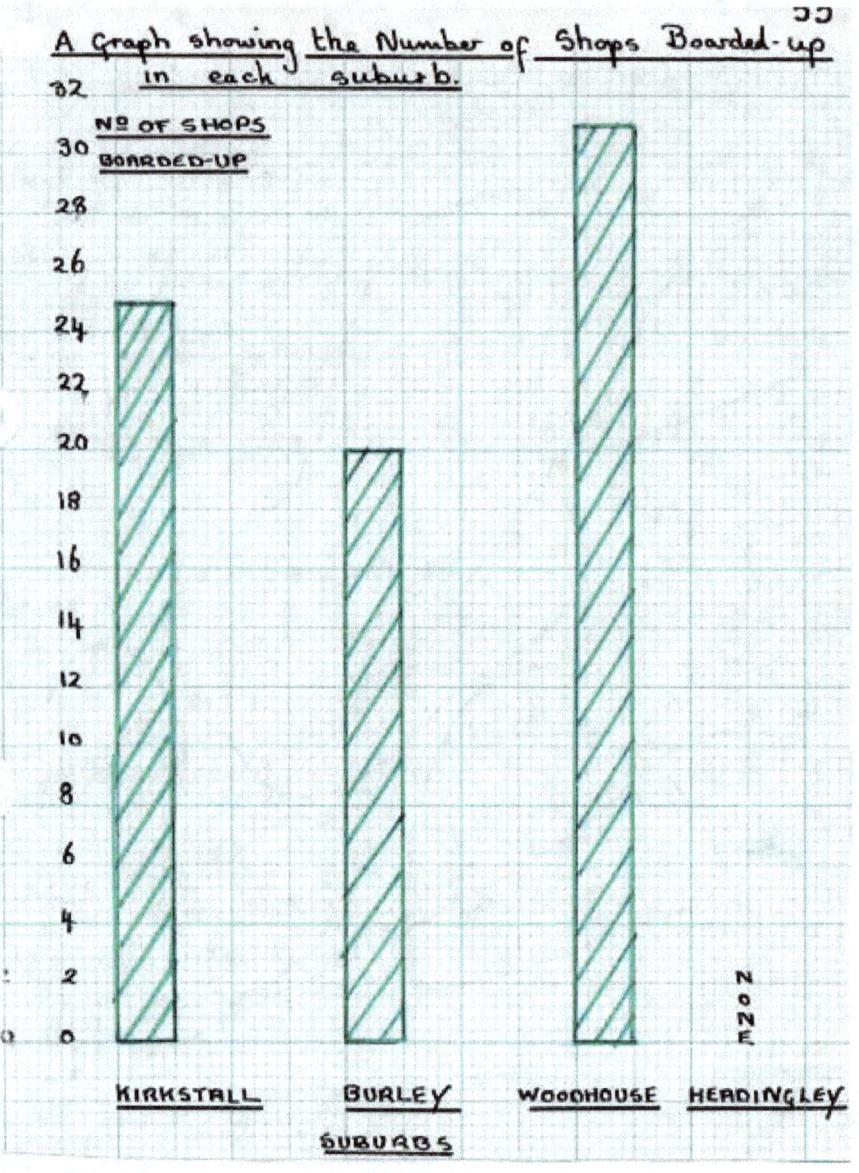

Map 54

Chapter 9: Conclusions

It is evident that each of the four suburbs is undergoing many changes in order to improve the industrial, social and living conditions. The most outstanding work in the period between 1949 and 1969 has been the large slum clearance scheme. Woodhouse has been the centre of attention for slum clearance since 1949; slum clearance is still in progress and many more houses in poor condition still remain and await demolition.

The greater part of the slum clearance has allowed rapid development of Education in Leeds. There have been extensions to the University-Hospital, formation of Central Colleges including Leeds Polytechnic which will form one large Educational Precinct. Housing development in Woodhouse is slow; where land has been cleared very little development has taken place. Some housing has been built in the form of multi-storey flats, having their own shopping areas. This type of housing does not occupy much ground space and they are amid open land. Demolition continues, eventually it will be a new residential suburb providing 18,000 homes.

It is Kirkstall that is now the centre of attention for slum clearance. We are aware of the plans for Kirkstall's industry but development has not begun yet. They are still clearing the slums and old factories. In the future Kirkstall should be a clean, modern light industrial Belt contributing its full share to the economy of Industrial Leeds. It will be void of that dense housing it had seen in the past.

Across the expanse of grassland, an amenity open space we have the residential area of Burley. This grassland separates the industrial area from the residential area. Burley too is undergoing re-development - they are general improvements to provide a better environment. It is the only suburb of the four where plans seem to be rather insignificant. It is also a suburb that has many problems because the suggested improvements are not sufficient to control the rapid decline of the terraced houses and the environment generally. The suburb will not achieve a better standard of living if the rate of influx of sudents, immigrants and large poor families is allowed to continue. As families move out of Burley, the student population, immigrants and large poor family communities move in and expand more and more. Although Burley is a re-development area, if no attention is given to the influx of these communities, then there will be no alternative but for Burley to sink further into decline and it will become the next slum area in this part of Leeds.

However these communities have to live somewhere and it is inevitable that these older parts of Leeds will eventually become slum areas simply because the housing does not come up to modern day requirements. It is Headingley where there has been the least slum clearance and the most development. The other three suburbs have kept their original roles, but Headingley has been given an entirely new role. Headingley in the past was a purely high class residential suburb but now thanks to the development and increased shopping facilities it has become the Main District Shopping Centre for a large area going beyond Headingley itself. The wealthy of Headingley have gradually moved further out of Leeds to newer and better parts of Leeds such as Adel and Alwoodley, leaving Headingley open to becoming a slowly declining suburb. It has already, to some extent, been submitted to University student and flat life. At the same time Leeds planners have made Headingley into a lively, busy and modern precinct serving an extensive district thus giving it prosperity.

To sum up, Kirkstall, Burley and Woodhouse, despite development and improvements will retain their original purposes: Kirkstall as a suburb for light industry, Burley and Woodhouse as residential suburbs. Woodhouse will become a new, modern suburb whereas Burley will continue to decline, so its future looks slightly uncertain. However, the suburb of Headingley having a new role will become an ever increasing sought after place to live, therefore its future seems more certain. Referring back to Map 27 the complete structure of the four suburbs can be seen.

Appendices

Place Names

HEADINGLEY: "A forest glade belonging to the Headda people" (from

Old English). This is significant inthe early topography and nature of English settlements.

WOODHOUSE: "Houses in a wood" (Anglo-Saxon). Again this is significant to the early settlement plan.

KIRKSTALL: "church-site". This is a reference to the monastery.

BURLEY: "A clearing near a fortification"

A brief look at the historical growth of Leeds

Leeds lies across the valley of the River Aire; it occupies the area where the valley widens.

In Anglo Saxon times, Leeds existed as a small nucleus, known as *Leodis*. It grew around a crossing of the River Aire which today is the Leeds bridge. Leeds was first mentioned in the Domesday Book of 1086 when it had a population of 300. By 1775 it had grown to a size of 17,000. Major expansions followed as a result of the turnpike roads, railway and canals as well as the great factory development, which took place during the Industrial Revolution.

The city spread quickly so housing accommodation for the population was urgently needed. Close-packed terraces of back to back houses were built over a large area. Between 1801 and 1901 the city's population increased eight times from 53,000 to 429,000. Industry was in the valleys and close to the radial road and railway system. The associated housing for the workers extended beyond that but it was also mixed with the industries themselves so that workers were near to their place of work. In 1948 Leeds had 90,000 houses of a total of 154,000 that were sub-standard and fit for demolition. The 90,000 houses included 54,000 back to back houses and 16,000 of these were built before 1844.

The problem of replacing these slum properties was aggravated by the general housing shortage. Council Estates began to spring up; the most ambitious post-war housing development took place in the Seacroft area, on the outskirts of Leeds. This century, the population has not risen greatly; it is now approximately half a million, but the extent of the built up residential suburbs has increased over the northern half of the city.

Relevant Plans and Acts for Leeds

Dr. FOWLERS PLAN 1821: High class residential area of the Park area was to be taken over by labourers, to build working class houses for workers at Gotts Mill.

LEEDS IMPROVEMENT ACT 1842: An Act passedto clear the parts of Leeds where slum property and inferior dwellings persisted. This Act has little effect. Back to backs were still being built at this time. The last back to back house was built in Leeds in 1937.

THE FIRST TOWN PLANNING ACT OF 1909: It gave the Leeds authorities the power to plan on areas of unbuilt land and also control where the houses should be built and also the amount of housing.

1934-1939 PLANNING ACT OF 1933: It proposed an extensive slum clearance scheme, abandoned due to the Second World War.

PLANNING ACT OF 1949 (1949-1961): It was designed to continue the extensive slum clearance scheme and launch the Post War housing developments to house the expanding population in areas – West Park, Moor Grange, Armley Heights. Private building began in Cookridge, Adel and Alwoodley. Modern plans for developments, forming "new" suburbs, namely Seacroft, Swarcliffe, and Whinmoor Estates.

1961-1981 TOWN PLANNING ACT: A review of the 1949-1961 Development Plan. Providing housing is the largest urban land use in the city, so housing has become the most important aspect in the urban renewal plans. It involves completion of the slum clearance scheme, new housing developments by the Corporation and Private sectors. There is also a great deal of re-development and rehabilitation affecting the older housing.

1960 UNIVERSITY ACT - THE CHAMBERLAIN PLAN: It aimed to "embrace the University, Infirmary and Maternity Hospital" into one traffic free precinct.

1963 REVIEW OF UNIVERSITY ACT: Extension Plans for the University to be increased to allow a larger intake of students.

The reasons for Kirkstall's industry and its development

Kirkstall is the only true Industrial suburb of the four under study and it has been industrial since the beginning of the 1100s.

In Norman Times, Leeds was a huge tract of land owned by the De Lacy Family. They built a castle at Ponteract to keep Leeds under observation so it the Delacies (meaning the Delacy family) who exercised much of the control over the land which makes up Leeds today.

Kirkstall Abbey was founded by a De Lacy in 1147, when after a serious ilness he thought a monastery and closeness to God would restore him. The Abbey was known as the Monastery of Headingley, but when the monks arrived they changed the name to Kirkstall, which means the site of a church. The monks were of the Cistercian order and were expert farmers. They did a great deal to develop agriculture in Yorkshire. The surrounding land was cleared of woods to make way for cattle and sheep rearing. Headingley was then known as Headingley Moor - it was an open grange belonging to the Abbey.

The monks reared sheep and cattle for the wool and hide industry, although it was still very much at a domestic level. The Abbey is situated close to the River Aire which was used in the cleaning processes of these industries. The monks also built a weir near the Abbey so they had water power from the River Aire too. So, domestic industry was set up in Kirkstall from as early as 1152.

Kirkstall Forge, a large prosperous engineering works of today is situated on the site of the original Kirkstall Forge which was founded by a group of dispossessed monks. The forge was probably "no larger than a sizeable Smithy" (quote by John Waddington Feather) and it was adjoined to the Aire which was their convenient source of power.

However, the "boom" of industry came to Kirkstall with the Industrial Revolution, because it had so many advantages to make it into a proper Industrial Area:

1. Industry of a domestic nature was already set up - there was

the wool industry, tanning and small iron and steel works.
2. The River Aire close by made it an already available and convenient source of power. The River was made navigable into Leeds at the end of the 17th Century.
3. The Leeds and Liverpool Canal was built in stages between 1770 and 1815 which encouraged industry and trade.
4. The vast railway network was built during this same period.
5. The ample means of transport for heavy goods such as coal and iron made it ideal for Heavy Industry. Unloading was easy, factories were built close to the River Aire on its immediate banks. Many large factories were built followed by dense housing to accomodate the workers. The houses were built around the factories. Gradually Kirkstall developed into a concentrated industrial mass - known as Intense industrialisation

Kirkstall Forge had been in the hands of the Earl of Cardigan but in 1779 during Industrialisation, John Butler and George Beacroft[1] (well known Industrialists of Leeds) took a lease on the forge and later extended and improved it.

The main types of industry that developed were the same as those pursued by the monks: iron and metal work, textiles and tanning. Industrialisation therefore did not change the type of industry but it changed the approach. Domestic industry turned into large scale factory industry. Kirkstall was a typical example of Industrialisation. The scene in Kirkstall today is basically the same although now most of the factories are exhausted and deteriorating. They are black and dirty with age, quite unsuitable for modern industry.

---

[1] J. Butler and G. Beacroft are both famous for their work in the development of Kirkstall as an industrial area. There are also a number of streets in Kirkstall named after them.

Leeds buildings protected from the bulldozers...

Fig 2.

St. Michael's Church, Headingley Lane, 1884.
St. Chad's Church, Otley Road, 1868. Early English style.
Old Bear Pit, Cardigan Road, 1840; formerly part of Leeds Zoological and Botanical Gardens.

WOODHOUSE AND WOODHOUSE LANE

St. Mark's Schoolhouse (old part), Raglan Road, 18th and 19th centuries.
Emmanuel Church (University Chaplaincy), 19th century, Early English style.
All Souls' Church, Blackman Lane, 1876-80. Early English style.
Nos. 15-18, Blenheim Terrace, late 18th century.
Lodges, Woodhouse Cemetery, early 19th century.
Mortuary Chapel at Woodhouse Cemetery, early 19th century.

ALWOODLEY

Moss Hall, Alwoodley Lane, date inscription 1363 over doorway.

SHADWELL

St. Paul's Church, 1841-2.
Manor Farmhouses, 18th century.
Barn at Manor Farm, 18th century.
Pigeon cote at Manor Farm, stonebuilt, mid-18th century.
No. 125, Main Street, small 17th century house.
Red Hall, 18th century, former private mansion now welfare hostel.
Pigeon cote at Red Hall, large square shaped and stone built.

CITY CENTRE FRINGE

Nos. 2, 3 and 4, Queen Square, late 18th century three-storey houses.
Springfield House, Hyde Terrace, 18th century, Leeds Roman Catholic Diocese Curial offices.
Woodsley Hall, Clarendon Road, 1837-40.
Hope Foundry, Mabgate, 1812.
Hope House, Mabgate, 19th century.
Springfield Mount, Priory of St. Wilfred's (Church of England Hostel of the Resurrection), 1908, brickbuilt with early Tudor form.
No. 16, Belmont Grove, 18th century two-storey brick house.
Denison Hall, Hanover Square, built 1786 for John Denison, now welfare hostel has three storeys with five bays in central block.

BURLEY

St. Margaret's Church, Cardigan Road, 1905-9.

HEADINGLEY

Kirkstall Grange, Beckett Park, 1752, with early 19th century alterations.

Acknowledgements

I would like to thank Mr Thirwall, the City engineer, and his assistant Mr. Rowling for allowing me to use various maps in their possession and providing me with some useful information. They were extremely helpful.

I would like to thank ThreePeppers Publishing for allowing this work to be printed after so many years.

Bibliography

- Leeds and its region, W. Beresford and G. R. J. Jones (1967)
- Leeds: The Heart of Yorkshire, John Waddington Feather (1967)
- Leeds City Council City Engineers and Town Planning Information Book (1961-1981), "Review of the Deveolpmennt Plan", C. G. Thirwall C. B. E. M. Eng.
- The Housing Problem, Hilary Rose (1968)
- A Guide to the City of Leeds: Approved by the Leeds City Council, G. C. Thirwall C. B. E. M. Eng.
- University of Leeds: Development Plan (1960)
- University of Leeds: Development Plan Review (1963)

www.ingramcontent.com/pod-product-compliance
Lightning Source LLC
Chambersburg PA
CBHW071517080526
44588CB00011B/1465